Patterns 2. Design, Art and Architecture

Patterns 2.
Design,
Art and
Architecture

Barbara Glasner, Petra Schmidt, Ursula Schöndeling (eds)

Birkhäuser
Basel · Boston · Berlin

Contents

Petra Schmidt
In the Maelstrom of Patterns
Introduction to the Second Volume

It was an open secret for years: anybody wanting to score a distinction at one of the many German design competitions should submit their product in black, white or, even better, silver. Whether you could indeed bag one of the desirable prizes, from the iF via Red Dot to the Design Award of the Federal Republic of Germany in that way, is another question, but it meant you were on the safe side, at least as far as style went. But for the last few years all that has been different. Along with colourful objects, patterned surfaces have now been turning up time and time again – on everyday objects like cell phones, for instance, and on furniture. Good design these days does not have to do without colour, or indeed pattern, any more. That goes for design competitions just as much as around the house. Wallpaper has come back home again to where design aficionados live. Retro patterns from the sixties are particularly sought after. It means that for a long while wallpaper has been more than just decoration for the wall. Instead it is in every interior highlight and eye-catcher: wallpaper is displayed like a picture or an artwork. And that is the new thing: showing patterns nowadays shows your "good taste".

That was not always the case. As Annette Tietenberg has already demonstrated in her essay "The Pattern Which Connects" for the first "Patterns" book, for more than a century the question of ornament in design and architecture had been, thanks to Adolf Loos and his essay "Ornament and Crime", a question of morality too. It was a case of categories, like "good" or "bad" taste. Educated people did not recognise any ornamental "prettification" of surfaces, but looked down on those areas of society, who spiced up their everyday life a bit with kitschy décor, be it round the coffee table or the wall cupboard in "Gelsenkirchen Baroque".[1]

Loos himself went further. "Cultural evolution equates to removing ornament from practical objects," as he declared in his 1908 essay. No wonder, then, that he tried to banish ornament out of Western habitats and into the South Pacific. The right place for such a regressive behaviour seemed to him to be with the tribes of Papua, whom he identified with licence and libidinousness. That was where superfluous ornament was justified; when all was said and done, the Papuans did tattoo themselves and even, according to Loos, ate their enemies. "Doing without ornament is a sign of intellectual strength. Modern people use the ornaments of earlier and foreign cultures as they see fit. They concentrate their own inventiveness on other things."

Patterns create Order
Patterns were, in contrast to ornament, a distinctly less "dangerous" attribute. They had, in fact, always embodied the principle of order, regardless of whether in biology, geometry or art history. Patterns are reliable. Repetitions following a pronounced rhythm are what denote patterns. And they never just counted as decoration or as ancillary embellishment; they were much rather considered as part of a structure. This very order is the very topic of "Patterns 2". While the first volume came across as a stocktaking or review on the subject of "Patterns in Design, Art, and Architecture", we as the editors of the second volume turned towards a specific aspect within patterns. In particular, we are interested in new abstract patterns as well as in patterns, where crystalline and foam-like structures make them seem to have their roots in nature. Naturally, this includes grids resuming the representation of constructivist art, and also structures bearing the traces of their digital origins. In his essay "Modernism – Setting the Pattern", Markus Zehentbauer (p. 8) discusses these topics more specifically.

One thing is clear: again and again during the course of art history, artists made use of geometrical and crystalline forms. We only need to think of Max Bill's paintings or of Bruno Taut's glass house. Today's take, however, is radically new. Once again, the architect Rem Koolhaas led the way. His Seattle Central Library, completed in 2003, possesses all previously mentioned attributes and praises a Modernism that presents itself as asynchronous, hard as glass and monumental. Koolhaas does without a distinct exterior appearance. Parallel shifting and mirroring causes new forms and impressions to come into view from every angle. The library seems like a bizarre crystalline mountain range, monolithic and untouchable. As a stimulus for the current delight in hard edges, i.e. crystallinism, the architecture critic Niklas Maak sees the famous Stealth Bomber, where the ephemeral design is clearly pragmatic. Proceeding from the fact that radar needs orthogonal surfaces to reflect off, the scientists at the Lockheed Corporation developed the canted exterior surfaces of the aeroplane in the 1980s. This engineering achievement impressed the designers too. Already in the nineties, this designing of a form basically intended to deconstruct itself caused a furore in the design community. Accordingly, the designer Tom Hardy opined enthusiastically on the contradiction "... that a machine designed not to be seen is so beautiful to look at!"

Loadbearing Patterns
At the Central Library in Seattle there is a peculiarity typical for patterns. Here they are namely not just embellishment or ornament, but also take on a function. They penetrate the

surface and combine with it. As already happened with Fuller's Geodesic Dome, the facetted pattern of the Central Library has become a bearing structure. The crystal lattice can carry load. No wonder. Because what the structure of crystal also stands for is, not least, hardness and stability. As we already know from diamonds, it distinguishes itself by its great density and durability and represents the most highly organised form of solid material.

A topic area that also interests artists. Dieter Detzner is one who explores the connection between order, chaos, chance and durability in his crystalline sculptures "Hans" and "Robert". With his pink-coloured sculpture "André", he investigates a special form of pattern: symmetry. The gleaming and self-reflecting structure is supposed to convey rigidity and order, regularity and security. He however adeptly counteracts this approach through his choice of colour and of a male first name as a title, which helps him break up the dominance and clarity of the symmetrical sculpture, lending it an almost "human" personality.

Patterns are not just order but also that means of distraction and pleasure that Loos tried to banish. They are suggestive. And, where order and clarity should actually prevail, they make things obscure. They are useless, irregular, diffuse, murky, enigmatic and erotic. Yet what Loos despised one hundred years ago is precisely what intrigues artists today. And so patterns are artistically interwoven, as in the paintings of Kevin Appel or Toby Ziegler. They are pleasurable and psychedelic when, as with Bjorn Copeland, they are combined into surreal scenarios or chaotic tableaux.

The art of disguising is also cleverly employed by the painters Matthias Bitzer and Igor Mischiyev who hide their subjects behind cascades of ornaments. Their patterns conceal and re-veal at the same time. Matthias Bitzer, for instance, has had models and semi-celebrities from art history, like the artist, prostitute, actor and co-founder of Dada, Emily Ball-Hennings disappear behind a veil of diamond shapes and geometrical patterns. He raises Emily out of historical obscurity to train a spotlight on her and her varied life. Yet at the same time he conceals her, veiling her with patterns.

How patterns are overlaid and layered on top of each other is the second major theme of this book. Birgit Dieker, for example, lays pattern upon pattern in her fabric sculptures so that she can subsequently excise and perforate the layers. It is actually not the fabrics but the patterns that are her material. She works with them like clay or stone and develops gloomy subjects, from skulls to riddled bodies. How she stitches diamond shapes together is quite decorous, but she interlaces them into a sort of maelstrom. That is how new constellations of patterns arise, real pattern-explosions.

Patterns overlay patterns. Whether they are cool, technical moirés, as by the photographer Liz Deschenes, or Tobias Rehberger's installations resembling room-dividers: patterns are stacked up, twisted round, interwoven and entangled. For his poster "Ki Ki Ri Ki", the Dutch graphic designer Harmen Liemburg lays classical subjects from the history of posters, like Hokusai's "The Great Wave off Kanagawa" or Bonnard's "France-Champagne", across each other in such a way that a new two-colour pattern emerges, which is reminiscent of the images in a Rorschach test. The designer understands how to use the most important works of his profession for his own purposes, to fashion new connections or respectively make his predecessors disappear in his pattern.

No other method represents the stimulating and suggestive effects of abstract patters as much as the psychoanalytical test based on the reading of blobs of ink developed in 1921 by the Swiss Gottfried Rorschach. A test person's immediate responses to the ink blob paintings were supposed to provide information on his or her emotional state. Can a pattern, itself obscure, reveal psychological problems? All that is controversial. Only one thing is clear: patterns are stimulating, suggestive and sometimes "wild". That nobody ever prohibited this "crime" is a really good thing!

1 Gelsenkirchen Baroque: After the wartime deprivations, large sectors of the German population were able to acquire some modest wealth. Their desire for a cosy security peaked in a style of furnishings that combined the rounded contours of Art Deco with the folk tradition of borders and ornamentation profiles. As these expansive pieces of furniture were more likely to be found among the working class, they rapidly became popularly known under the title of "Gelsenkirchen Baroque". The city of Gelsenkirchen stands here as a synonym for coal mining and for the miners employed in the collieries.

Markus Zehentbauer
Modernism – Setting the Pattern

You can still find them in the toys sections of our department stores and on Christmas Markets – cardboard cylinders containing mirrors and bits of coloured glass. Even today, when kaleidoscopes are cheap items made in China, those looking through the lens are still captured by the magic of these optical devices so excessively popular in 19th-century Europe and the United States. You gaze into a different world, a colourful and abstract one that you can change any time you like: as you turn the kaleidoscope, reflecting and diffracting light constantly creates new, symmetrical patterns – and just as they fall apart, so new ones emerge. In contrast to other optical devices, the kaleidoscope does nothing more than serve our visual pleasure – it may be an anachronism, but it does provide us with a nice image for the kaleidoscopic aesthetics of our times. They are continuously changing, above all on their – material and immaterial – surfaces, where patterns play a predominant role. These emphasise the surface and titillate the eyes; they attract our gaze and hold it. However, today's patterns don't restrict themselves to covering surfaces, they also reach out spatially; they do not only decorate objects and buildings and give them structure, they have become the basis for constructing and organising new objects.

In recent years, the Berlin artist Olafur Eliasson has constructed several walk-in kaleidoscopes, transferring the effects of these optical devices to installations which you can justifiably call works of art as much as architecture or design. The latest version of these was created in 2007 for an exhibition in the San Francisco Museum of Modern Art: Eliasson's "One-way Colour Tunnel" has a complex, prism-like wall structure generated by light, colour and glass; its shimmering, three-dimensional patterns make you dizzy when you walk through them. It is a work of art that only comes about as its observers move. Eliasson is heading a new generation of artists, designers and architects, who are making use of patterns in their design processes. He reconstructs both optical and physical phenomena from nature, from scientific models and from templates from art history and so draws on the most diverse of sources. Eliasson has conjured up fogs; he has had a sun rise in the Tate Modern; he has erected grottos, and in 2007, in cooperation with the architect Kjetil Thorsen, he designed a spiral pavilion for the Serpentine Gallery in London. The spiral, too, is a pattern. It originates in three forms: in nature, it exists in the form of snails; then it serves as a scientific model to visualise, for instance, growth periods in plants; and finally it is a highly artificial phenomenon. All these aspects – nature, science and art – coalesce in the pattern.

But what exactly is a pattern? And how does it come into being? Basically, anything and everything can become a pattern, as long as it is repeated – the repetition of identical or similar elements and motifs is the central criterion for a pattern; the more regular and more symmetrical the repetition, the easier it is to recognise. In contrast to the ornament, which embellishes a façade, pieces of porcelain or a canvas and which is always connected to its medium, the pattern is an abstract construct not bound to a particular function. Designers, artists and architects make use of it. In science, it turns up in the visualisation of repeated values, and we can observe it in all manner of forms in nature. Despite this, the term ornament is often used instead of pattern.[1] The reason why lies in the influential reception of Adolf Loos's essay "Ornament and Crime". First published in 1908, it is still the best-known modern text on the topic – even though, or perhaps because, it generates a moral impetus to express the author's rejection of any ornament, whether applied to buildings or functional objects. The view that ornaments or patterns respectively are the antithesis to Modernity is still alive today. However, on examining them closely, the two have more in common than you might think.

With his 2001 exhibition "Ornament and Abstraction" in the Fondation Beyeler, Markus Brüderlin undertook the as yet most extensive attempt at revising our image of an ornament-free Modernity. However, he still provides his most crucial propositions with question marks – such as the one as to whether viewing 20th-century abstract painting from a particular angle should be understood as a continuation of the history of ornamentation.[2] All the more convincing is the way the curator Markus Brüderlin traces how the arabesque progressed from being an Arabian tendril ornament to become an abstract motif in painting and central to the image: in the 19th century, at a time of crisis for the ornament, the arabesque broke away from its purely decorative function and found its way into painting, giving critical impulses for the development of abstraction as a pictorial element that can shift from the floral-naturalistic to the linear-abstract, from the representational to the non-representational. The arabesque appears in Henry van de Velde's und Josef Hoffmann's works; for Kupka, Kandinsky and Mondrian it constitutes a new, self-representational image structure. However, the exhibition in the Fondation Beyeler also demonstrated how the term ornament does not lend itself to tracing the line of non-representational painting from the Second World War to today. The pictorial concepts of constructive and concrete art, of works by Frank Stella or Sol LeWitt, of the Neo-Geo-painters or of contemporary artists re-appropriating the geometrical models of Modernism, do not derive from ornaments but are based rather on structures, on grids – that is to say, on patterns.

Patterns were once the most important form of ornament – well into the 19th and even the 20th century. This is not to say that Modernism – in its search for pure and absolute form, on the one hand, and with its penchant for strict functionalism on the other – excluded them: quite the opposite, in fact. Geometrical patterns, in particular, represent some of the most crucial categories in Modernism. Its concern with surfaces was one of the preconditions for overcoming illusionism and for forcing painting to concentrate on them – and it made autonomy possible in painting. In the 1950s and 1960s, artists like Max Bill and Karl Gerstner made use of a second aspect – namely the fact that patterns are based on comprehensible structural principles and, as a rule, do not have an author – in order to pursue their goal of an art that can be rendered objective and is based on universal rules. And not least: the fundamental principle of repetition inherent in patterns is the fundamental principle of Modernism itself. This now includes design and architecture too: Pop Art defines itself through repetitions; the adding-up of identical elements, free of any hierarchy and striving for infinity, reappears in the All-over, whilst functionalist systems like grids and modules also produce patterns. We only need to think of the composite posters designed by Almir Mavignier in the 1960s, the actual pattern effect of which does not unfold until they are placed above and next to each other.

There is indeed a continuity of patterns in Modernism – and beyond it. It is not restricted to seemingly anecdotal exceptions to the rule – such as teachers and students at the Bauhaus designing wallpaper, which was traded extremely successfully under the label "Bauhaus-Tapeten" (Bauhaus wallpaper). Or the fact that Loos, of all people, used green Cipollino marble, with its richly contrastive structure, for filling the empty spaces in his agenda-setting house on Michaeliplatz in Vienna. As early as 1965, the curators of the exhibition "ornament without ornament?" in Zurich and Munich had realised to what extent patterns also put their mark on the surfaces of industrial culture. "Ornamental patters often serve as vehicles of visual stimuli, yet the effect of the material used or its texture do so equally often, in fact, they are two substitutes for ornament," the catalogue declares.[3] Photos document what the curators had discovered on their stroll through our modern world: patterns from the soles of shoes, drain covers, the paving of roads, corrugated iron and steel skeletons. What might seem like superficial and formalistic observations, is, however, not to be dismissed lightly.

The modernistic material aesthetics, also concealed in the term "purism", did not simply result in smooth and empty surfaces. Designers and architects displayed the structures of their materials, the grain of stone and of exotic kinds of wood, craquelé glazing on porcelain, and wickerwork. Another modern pattern is as functional as it is aesthetic: one of holes. In 1938, Hans Coray perforated his chair for the Schweizer Landesausstellung (Swiss National Exhibition) so that rain water could drain away and to reduce weight even further; in Braun appliances from the 1950s and 1960s patterns of holes in regular lines indicate the location of loudspeakers and ventilation. Of much more consequence, however, was the way architects and designers as well as artists systematised design as such – and how, in doing this, they made use of the fundamental rules of repetition, which often lead to the creation of patterns. We are talking about working with modules, with series and grids that simplify and rationalise design and production processes. As early as in the 1920s, for instance, prefabricated concrete components were used in the construction of the "New Frankfurt" settlements; the respective modules were aimed at the "New Man". The best known example for this, Le Corbusier's Modulor, illustrates how the creation of a mathematical order was the ultimate goal: Le Corbusier set out from the measurements of the human body and was guided by the golden mean in order to generate a sequence of further necessary proportions. The façade itself displays his system of proportions as a pattern; later, the free patterns of curtain façades and grid façades come to dominate. Consumer objects, by their very definition, follow the rule of the series. It is only serial industrial production that transforms a plan into design, and this process not only includes concepts of rationalisation, but an aesthetic component as well. For the individual object is always part of a system, one of many identical objects, and it is staged as such: modern product photography shows stacked crockery, stacking chairs in stacks, modular furniture systems in all possible versions – seriality is always there somewhere.

Supported by scientific and mathematical models and methods that were also taken up by art, the systematisation and rationalisation of design reached its peak in the 1960s at the Hochschule für Gestaltung (Academy for Design) in Ulm. Many of the geometric structures from concrete art go back to mathematical processes, which create patterns – permutations, progressions, reflections – geometry as beauty, as universal order and as a universally comprehensible method. At the Bauhaus, the constructivists and the masters like Kandinsky and Klee were already arguing among themselves about the differences between composition and construction, between images that were laid down individually and subjectively and those that arose according to seemingly objective methods and rules. "Nothing is more concrete, more real than a line, a colour, a surface," writes Theo van Doesburg in 1930 in his manifesto on concrete art.[4] Accordingly, concrete painters bet on the immediate effect of their pictorial methods, which were not intended to represent anything but themselves. The result: sequences, grids, lattices, symmetries and line paintings, which displayed not only their geometrical shapes clearly and unambiguously, but also how they were created. According to a much-quoted axiom by the Swiss painter Richard Paul Lohse, who, like Karl Gerstner, became known for his colour grid paintings, "the method is the picture". There are paintings by the protagonist and theoretician of concrete art, Max Bill, which have such explanatory titles like "rotation of equal amounts of paint around white centres" or "field of six merging colours". Here, series played an important role, as they allowed you to demonstrate the many different versions possible from a particular ordering principle, from a particular method.

Frank Stella and Sol LeWitt and the protagonists of Op Art made use of anonymous geometrical patterns in an even more radical way. Stella filled the surface of his paintings with patterns of regular bands of colour, always identical and running parallel to the shape of the canvas. An All-over that doesn't require any design decisions anymore, so it results in a picture perceived much rather as an object. And LeWitt placed the idea, the verbalised concept of an artwork, above its execution and had his image and spatial structures carried out by others. The protagonists of Op Art went down an entirely different path, which is receiving a lot of attention again today. They jumbled up strict, ordering rules from concrete art and confused the eye of the observer by creating optical effects like after-images and moiré. Their goal was to challenge the audience and consequently to involve them more strongly – with a complexity that already points towards today's development of patterns.

Why tell this long history? It is necessary for an understanding of how designers, architects and artists today make use of patterns. They don't just, as was still the case a few years ago, turn to traditional ornaments, to those books of patterns that were widely distributed well into the 19th century and were being reprinted in some cases.[5] The often-expressed notion that the return of the pattern means a return to craft doesn't accord with the current situation, either. Apart from the fact that, rather than talking about a return to the history of the pattern, one should talk about its continuation, it overlooks the further fact that the appearance of designed objects in crafts is often brought about only by the use of new technologies. Intarsia work, engravings, reliefs, cutting and polishing can be generated digitally today:[6] Tord Boontje has filigree garlands cut out of sheet metal with a high-tech, precision cutter or has them etched in with a photo-engraving technique; Moroso has also developed a computer-guided cutting process for his textiles with their blocked-out flower ornamentation. The patterned designs of Marcel Wanders and Patricia Urquiola are

all of them not applied any differently. And because you can use computer-guided machines like CNC mortising equipment, originally intended for mass production, just as well to produce the limited editions and one-offs so sought after today, author-designers can apply this trend without having to use a horde of craftsmen. What looks like a retrospect on the 19th century, that only masks the fact that in design there has for a while now been a noticeable inclination towards geometrical patterns, towards prismatically dissected surfaces, lattice and web structures and towards crystalline forms, where the digital process of development itself finds expression as well. One point of reference here are the 1960s too, although not the design of those years, but their art and architecture. To take one instance: the London studio Barber Osgerby can evince how its ceramic walls for the stores of the Stella McCartney fashion label unabashedly cite façades from sixties department stores.

What is happening at the moment is a renaissance of geometrical patterns from the spirit of Modernism. Today's designers draw from the most diverse sources; they do not stop at the boundaries of their discipline and they merge their materials so skillfully that something new arises. A generation of artists had already discovered geometrical Modernism for itself: the concept of Neo Geo, introduced in the 1980s to denote a few New York painters like Philip Taaffe and Peter Halley, has remained current. At that time, Donald Baechler was quoting Malevich, just like the German Imi Knoebel – albeit the former with unabashed irony and the latter with serious constructivist purpose. The second wave, which refers particularly to the 1960s, has now embraced all design disciplines, including fashion and graphic design. In art, we call it "Formalism"[7] or "New Constructivism"[8] and with it we combine all possible directions, which then form an opposing current to the extreme success of figurative art. It is scarcely surprising that in 2006 the German artist Tomma Abts won the Turner Prize for her small scale, geometrical paintings.

Neo Neo Geo is difficult to pin down, and that is exactly what basically defines it. It ranges from Bernd Ribbeck's delicate, small-scale ballpoint pictures through Christine Streuli's suggestive pattern-samples to works by Jim Lambie and Jim Isermann, which take up entire rooms and comprehensively cover walls, ceilings, floors and steps with such startling patterns that they make you dizzy. We can see how enthusiastically the artists have adopted the concepts and theories of Modernism, yet they are not interested in its rules and dogmas. Bernd Ribbeck's pictures, produced with felt tip pens, ballpoint and permanent markers, do indeed point clearly to their constructivist models, yet they can just as easily topple into psychedelia, even into the esoteric, with their perfect symmetries and staged lighting effects. This phenomenon is noticeable with other artists who work with patterns, Rorschach effects and origami. Collages made out of geometrical patterns and representational models are equally conspicuous. Matthias Bitzer, for instance, overlays historical watercolour portraits with constructivist quotations and symmetrical patterns, in order to create space for a story. It is rare for artists to restrict themselves to a purely geometrical gesture, one seeking after ideal forms – they allude to other stories, imbue their pictures with surprising contents, if they do not simply adopt them. In this way Dieter Detzner quotes an artistic trope, the metaphysical magic of which motivated Modernism a hundred years ago: the crystal. Architects like Bruno Taut and painters like Erich Heckel and Lyonel Feininger recognised in it the symbol for their holistic ideas. On the one hand, the crystal is a mystical object; on the other, pure form; it reveals the inner laws of nature and is, in the same way, an abstract structure, the symmetries of which are composed of ideal polyhedrons, absorbing and reflecting light. The crystal, therefore, stands as a catalyst between naturalism and abstraction, as it were, between representing the first and also the second, inner nature. A construct that is gaining new significance today, at the onset of an age when nature can be technically reproduced.

By contrast, the pattern of the target, consisting of different sized circles, has an unequivocally cultural origin. Jasper Johns introduced this everyday but iconic sign into his abstract painting, and here it varies between representation and abstraction. Since Johns, the ambiguous image of the target has made repeated appearances as a pictorial motif: the Danish artist Poul Gernes has been painting target pictures all his life, and in 2007 Jacob Dahlgren covered a wall completely with real dartboards, at which you could throw real darts. An object made of patterns or a pattern made of objects? It is both, Dahlgren would probably say, and he also reproduces abstract patterns from art history in mural installations with bathroom scales, kitchen sponges and yoghurt pots.

A target or, even more elementary, a chessboard, are both simple patterns, and how they have come about is easy to understand. As already mentioned, patterns arise through repeating the same and similar elements, for example, circles with a growing diameter or squares, from which an orthogonal grid emerges. Such regular symmetrical patterns represent order, perfection and beauty. But how do you generate more complex patterns? What is decisive is how the selected individual elements, and the methods for repeating or combining them respectively, correspond – the most frequent methods would be mirror images, together with rotations and parallel shifts. Here, so-called tessellations play a vital role. The

technique involved is concerned with dismantling polygons, whilst the name itself can be understood as meaning: "to cover with a pattern". The point is to fill a surface with elements all the same size without overlapping and gaps. Researchers have found out that regular tessellations are only possible using three different forms: with squares, triangles and hexagons. However, the possible number of all the irregular tessellation groups, like those Richard Buckminster Fuller used in 1967 for his pavilion at the Montreal Expo, is that much greater.

Recently a trend has emerged to asymmetrical, dynamic and voluminous patterns, which go far beyond the models from the sixties. People can achieve correspondingly complex structures with, for instance, those techniques of paper folding mostly termed origami. In this way, the English artist and designer Richard Sweeney uses nothing more than cutting and folding to create dense symmetrical objects so complex that no one can replicate how they are made any more.

Classical patterns, many of which can be found in the Alhambra in Grenada, for instance, can be calculated mathematically. Meanders, spirals, undulations, zigzags – all these can be formulated. Other constellations of patterns have, however, only been discovered in the course of the 20th century, such as fractals and the Penrose pattern. In 1975, the French mathematician Benoît Mandelbrot recognised the principle of a geometrical pattern created from self-similar forms, the characteristics of which do not change with scaling. That is, for example, the case when an object consists of several reduced copies of itself. What has subsequently served scientists and scholars in describing irregular, splintered, even chaotic forms in nature has been picked up by artists in order to generate new patterns. In 1974, the mathematicians Roger Penrose and Robert Ammann then again discovered a pattern with which you can fill a surface up completely without having to repeat a basic sequence periodically. The best-known example derives from nothing more than two differently formed rhombuses, which offer an irregular pattern yet one infinitely extendable across a surface.

Whilst patterns in art are still mostly sampled, drawn, carved and sawn or folded by hand, they have long been generated digitally in design and in architecture. What does that mean exactly? What we see on a computer screen are the visual representations of endlessly repeated calculations – graphics, therefore, and behind them lie concealed data and algorithms, which are paradoxically meant to be seen all the same as naturalistic representations. That also means they are never the inevitable result of any particular data, but always only one of many possible versions.[9] It is not surprising that visualising calculations in this way immediately produces patterns out of dots (pixels) and lines. The pioneers of computer art already took advantage of that, for instance Herbert W. Franke, who transposed music and sequences of movement, among other things, into graphics on the screen and depicted procedures such as rotation. Current CAD design programs initially arise from geometrical patterns: anybody producing digital 3-D objects can employ wire mesh models, which are structured out of lines and curves and have facetted surfaces made up of three or four cornered polygons, onto which textures, that is, rendered surfaces, can be projected. You can manipulate, distort, twist and mirror the models. And in similar fashion, so-called parametric modelling, for example, with numbers, geometrical figures and formulae lead onto geometrical patterns. But it is only since we coupled it all to computer controlled production machines (through Computer Aided Manufacturing, CAM) that we can translate digital designs directly out of the virtual and into the real without any analogue intermission. This development has not only altered the general design process fundamentally but also the way patterns work.

More and more designers and architects find the forms of their designs exclusively in the virtual. They initiate a process of generating structures without any possible result in prospect and they monitor this process until a solution is found. Borrowing from biology, we have meanwhile come to refer to "morphogenesis"[10]. The parameters applied ensure that even the support structures are freely adaptable. In this way, subtle dynamic forms arise, which would not be possible without the new tools. Patterns play a decisive and fundamental role here: they are no longer applied subsequently but are integrated into the construction of buildings, or they form themselves the principle governing construction and organisation, out of which a building then arises. That is very easy to recognise with Herzog & de Meuron's Olympic Stadium in Beijing, where a comprehensive meshwork is structure, surface and space all at the same time. Seldom has anyone come so close to Gottfried Semper's notion that the origin of architecture lies in weaving and interlacing. The precise construction derives from a research team at the ETH Zurich and their programming of a structure with 600 variables and an evolutionary algorithm, which is meant to prevent any substantial gaps arising. The result: a drawing made up of a hundred lines, which cannot be rendered by hand.[11] Chris

Bosse used a completely different pattern for the Olympic swimming stadium next door. He derives an irregular geometrical structure from the aggregate mass, foam, which he adapted with air bags – a translucent, highly communicative exterior. Since we have actually been able to translate into reality the design programs' perfection as drafts, patterns have become independent. They no longer restrict themselves to organising and structuring surfaces. No, they set the latter in motion, separate from them and achieve a suggestive power first indicated in the sixties. Patterns can be highly complex today, asymmetrical, full of perspectival distortion and permanently mutable – that makes them not just an expression of a new digital aesthetic but of our times as well. Anyone going past buildings by Herzog & de Meuron or through installations by Olafur Eliasson is in for an interesting experience: the patterns are ceaselessly changing and yet they can be continued infinitely. A comprehensive continuum arises, which eliminates old-fashioned principles like the separation of walls and roofs – and has only been possible through computerisation. Artists like Tobias Rehberger and Jim Isermann also use patterns in this way: as a construction principle, with which you can create rhythmic-dynamic installations and extend them at will. Ronan and Erwan Bouroullec can even make do with a single basic element for building spatial sculptures, spatial partitions or complete spaces: their North Tiles are textile modules the size of tiles, which can be very easily and imaginatively combined. They are no use as individual elements but only gain a function through being combined – even if, as in the case of the Rocs produced for the Vitra Edition, nothing more than a sculpture comes out of it. Modules were once a Modernist principle, which were meant to systematise design. Yet the Bouroullecs' modules do not celebrate norms as a means of rationalising individual forms of living. Their interlocking units are not committed to any purpose and represent an invitation to free-ranging creativity. You can take the patterns of this module system apart at any time and recombine them into other forms and divide up space with them. But, above all, you are meant to enjoy what you have created yourself: the sequence of colours, the constellation and, not least, the patterns.

Markus Zehentbauer, born in 1971, is an editor with the design magazine "form". He studied art history in Munich, then worked at the Museum für Konkrete Kunst Ingolstadt and for several years wrote for various sections of the "Süddeutsche Zeitung".

1   See Farshid Moussavi, Michael Kubo, The Function of Ornament, Barcelona 2006.
2   Exhibition catalogue Ornament und Abstraktion, Riehen 2001, p. 12.
3   Exhibition catalogue ornament ohne ornament?, Zürich 1965, p. 43.
4   Theo van Doesburg, quoted and translated from: Willy Rotzler, "Annäherung an das Konkrete", in: Peter Volkwein (ed.), Museum für Konkrete Kunst Ingolstadt, Heidelberg 1993, p. 47.
5   See David Batterham, World of Ornament, Cologne 2006.
6   See Annette Tietenberg, "Das Muster, das verbindet", in: Petra Schmidt, Annette Tietenberg, Ralf Wollheim (eds), Patterns – Muster in Design, Kunst und Architektur, Basel, Boston, Berlin 2005, p. 92.
7   Title of an exhibition in the Kunstverein in Hamburg, 9.10.2004 – 9.1.2005.
8   Title of an exhibition in the Bielefelder Kunstverein, 24.8. – 21.10.2007.
9   See Claus Pias, "Punkt und Linie zum Raster – Zur Genealogie der Computergrafik", in: Exhibition catalogue, Riehen 2001, p. 66ff.
10   See Hubertus Adam, "Schöne neue Welten, Architektur im Zeitalter der Digitalisierung", Neue Zürcher Zeitung, 24.3.2007, p. 71.
11   See Ludger Hovestadt, "Strategien zur Überwindung des Rasters", in: archithese 4, 2006, p. 84.

Hitoshi Abe
PTK Pachinko Tiger, Sendai, Miyagi prefecture, Japan, 2005
Games hall
Façade design: Asao Tokolo

15 **Hitoshi Abe**

PTK Pachinko Tiger, Sendai, Miyagi prefecture, Japan, 2005

Games hall
Façade design: Asao Tokolo
above: Detail by night
below: Detail by day

16   **Anni Albers**

Yellow Meander, 1970

Screenprint, 71.1 x 61 cm

© The Josef and Anni Albers Foundation/2008, ProLitteris, Zurich

Anni Albers
Red Meander II, 1970–71
Screenprint, 71.1 x 61 cm
© The Josef and Anni Albers Foundation/2008, ProLitteris, Zurich

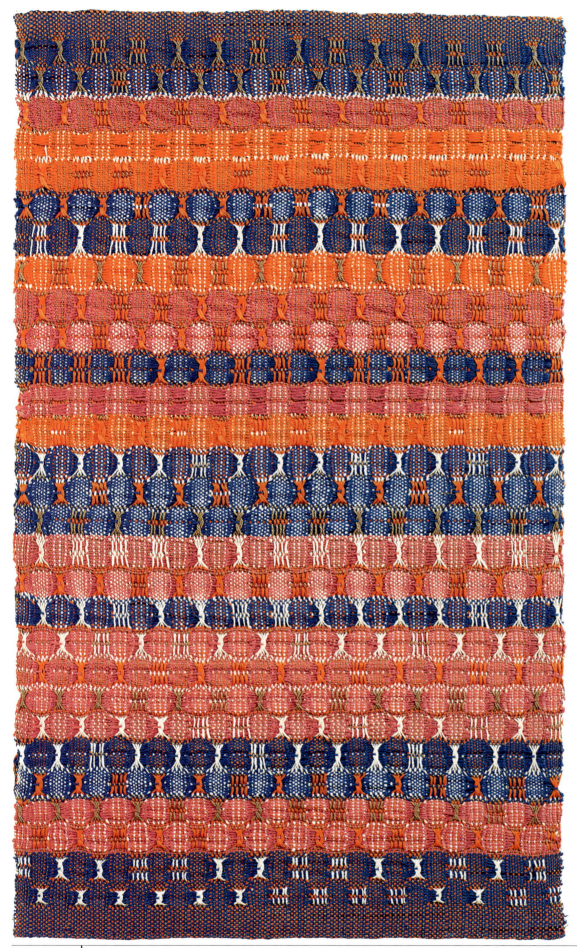

18 **Anni Albers**
Red and Blue Layers, 1954

Cotton, 61 x 36.8 cm
Collection of the Josef and Anni Albers Foundation
© The Josef and Anni Albers Foundation/2008, ProLitteris, Zurich

19

Anni Albers

Intersecting, 1962
Cotton and rayon, 40 x 42 cm
Private collection
© The Josef and Anni Albers Foundation/2008, ProLitteris, Zurich

Nikos Alexiou
The End, Greek Pavilion, Venice Biennale 2007, 1995–2007
Paper cuts, projection, digital prints

Nikos Alexiou

The End, Greek Pavilion, Venice Biennale 2007, 1995–2007

Paper cuts, projection, digital prints
View of installation

23 | **Nikos Alexiou**
The End, Greek Pavilion, Venice Biennale 2007, 1995–2007
Paper cuts, projection
Detail

Nikos Alexiou
Monastery of Iviron, 2003/2004
Paper cut, 735 x 714 cm, Sala Alcala 31, Madrid, 2004
View of installation
Courtesy of Françoise Heitsch, Munich

Nikos Alexiou

Monastery of Iviron, 2003/2004

Paper cut, 238 x 980 cm, European Patent Office Munich
View of installation
Courtesy of Françoise Heitsch, Munich

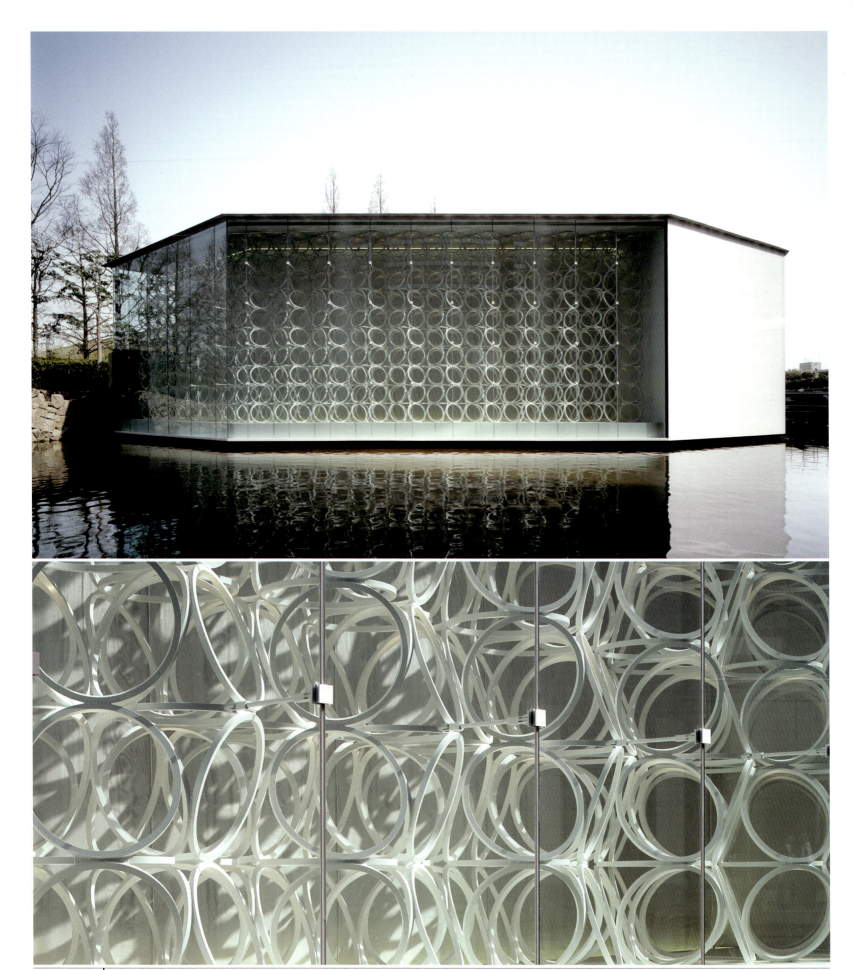

Jun Aoki

White Chapel, Hyatt Regency Hotel, Osaka, 2005–06

Wedding chapel
above: Exterior view
below: Detail of façade structure

Jun Aoki
White Chapel, Hyatt Regency Hotel, Osaka, 2005–06
Wedding chapel
above: Interior view
below: Detail of façade structure

Jun Aoki

White Chapel, Hyatt Regency Hotel, Osaka, 2005–06

Wedding chapel
Exterior views by night

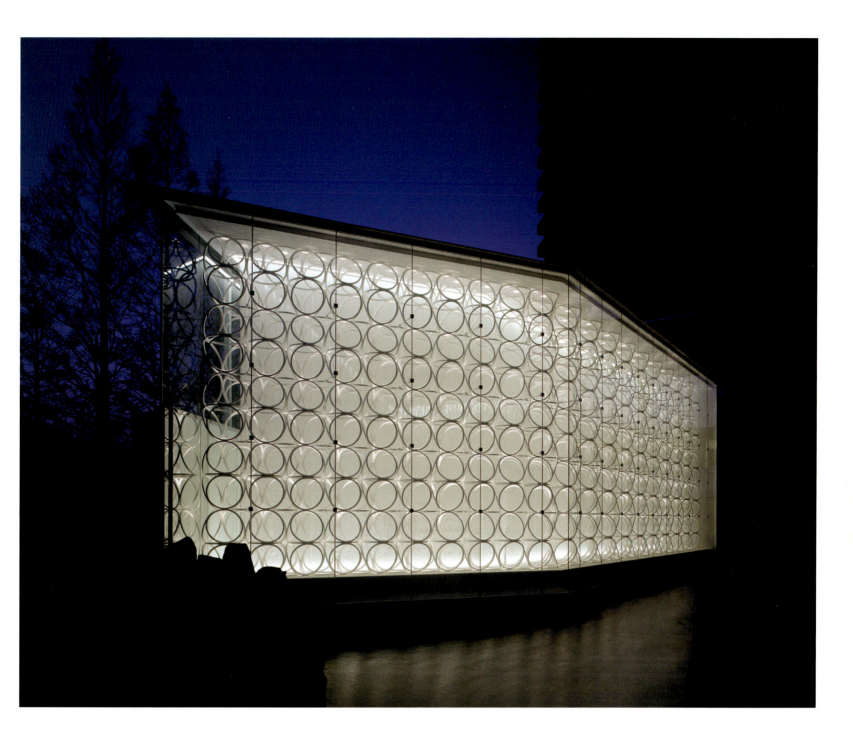

Kevin Appel
County Home I, 2006
Oil, enamel and acrylic on canvas with panels, 183 x 185.5 cm
Courtesy of Wilkinson Gallery, London

Kevin Appel
Little Flower, 2006
Oil, enamel and acrylic on canvas with panels, 203.5 x 211 cm
Courtesy of Wilkinson Gallery, London

Kevin Appel
Country Home #4 (Dreamer), 2006
Oil, enamel and acrylic on canvas with panels, 203 x 195.5 cm
Courtesy of Wilkinson Gallery, London

Kevin Appel
Untitled, 2006
Oil, enamel and acrylic on canvas with panels, 99.5 x 92 cm
Courtesy of Wilkinson Gallery, London

34 **Neil Banas**
Rain, 2007
Idealised landscape simulation, created using the programming language
"Processing"

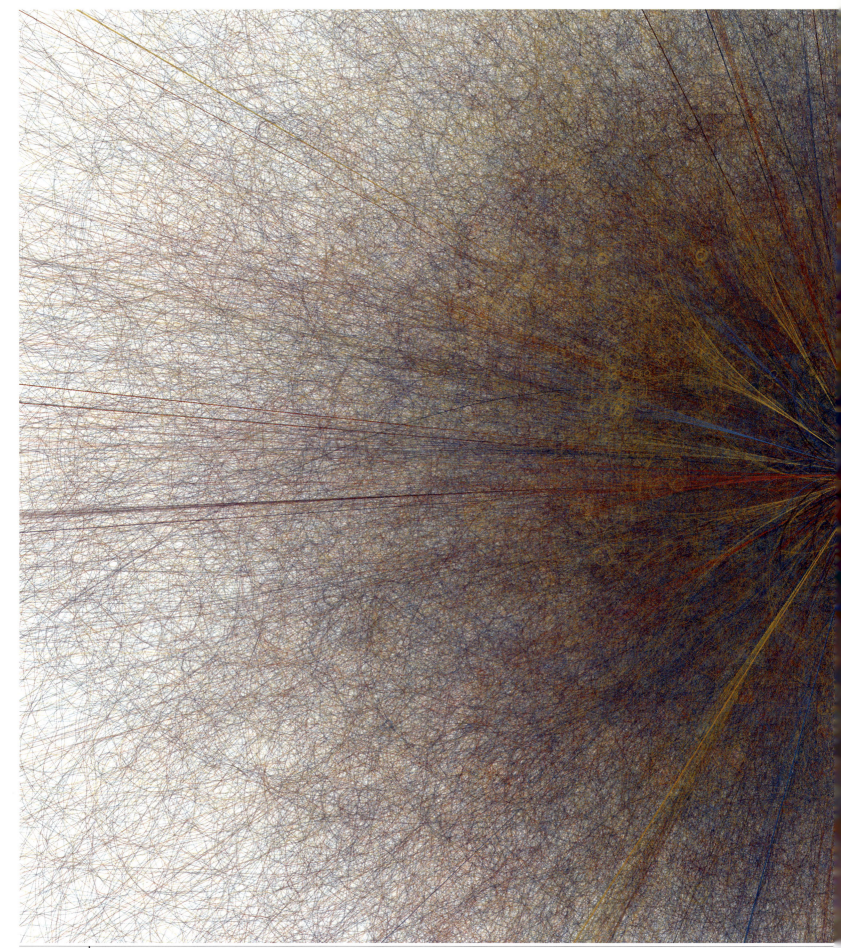

36

Neil Banas
Rosette 80, 2007
Simulation of clusters of plantlike shoots, created using the programming language
"Processing"

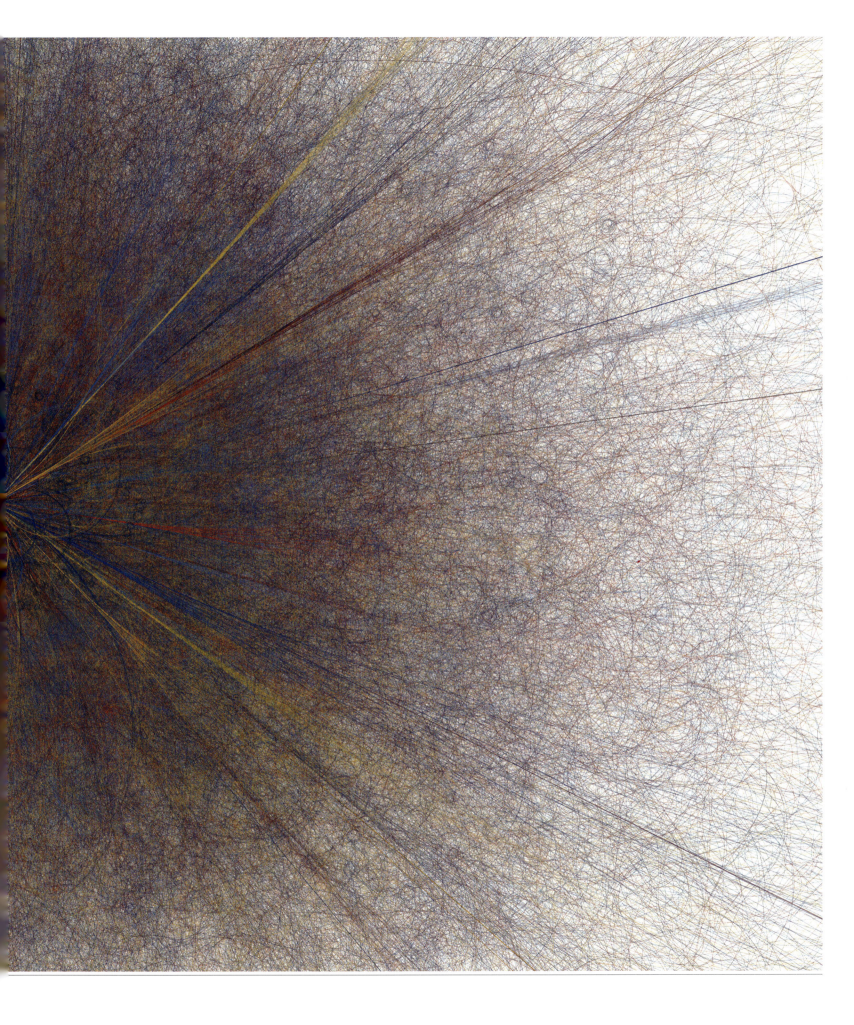

Barber Osgerby
Stella McCartney store, 2002 (Interior view)
3D ceramic tiles
Manufacturer: Team Work Italia

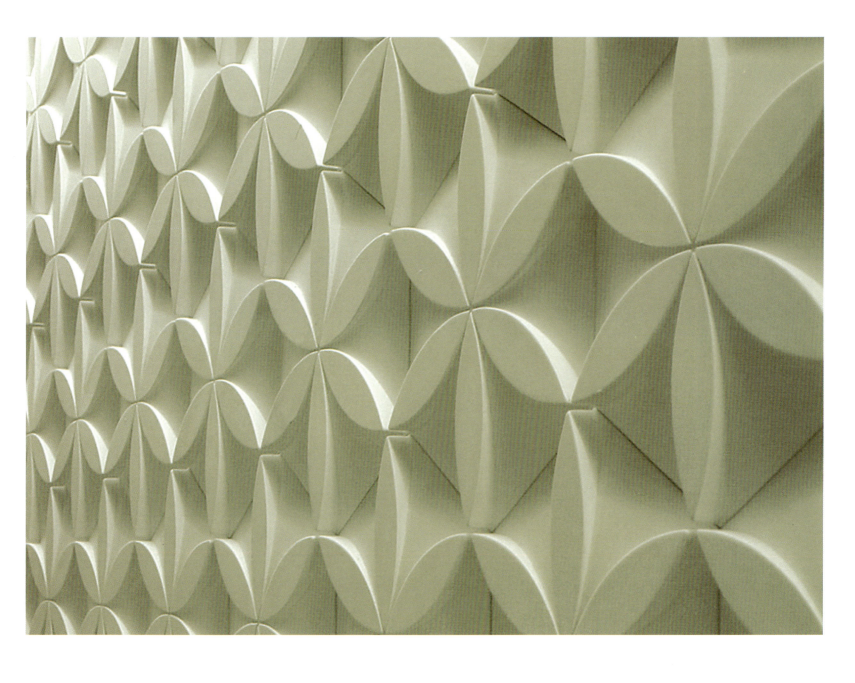

39 | **Barber Osgerby**
Stella McCartney store, 2002 (Detail)
3D ceramic tiles
Manufacturer: Team Work Italia

40   **Barber Osgerby**
Starflower Brown, 2007
Hand-knotted rug made from Tibetan wool, 274 x 183 cm
Manufacturer: The Rug Company

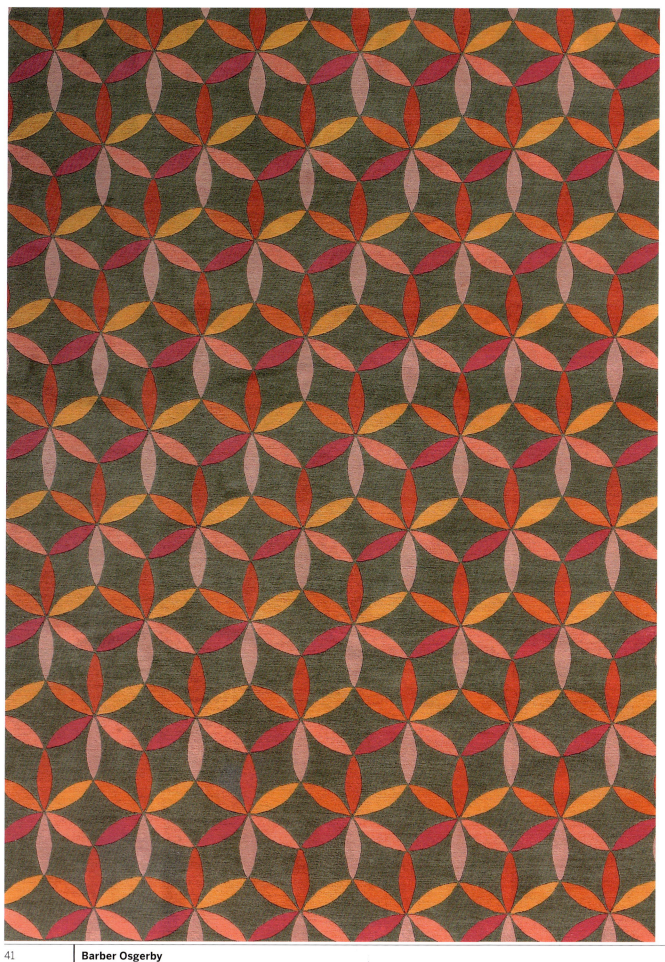

41 **Barber Osgerby**
Starflower Pink, 2007
Hand-knotted rug made from Tibetan wool, 274 x 183 cm
Manufacturer: The Rug Company

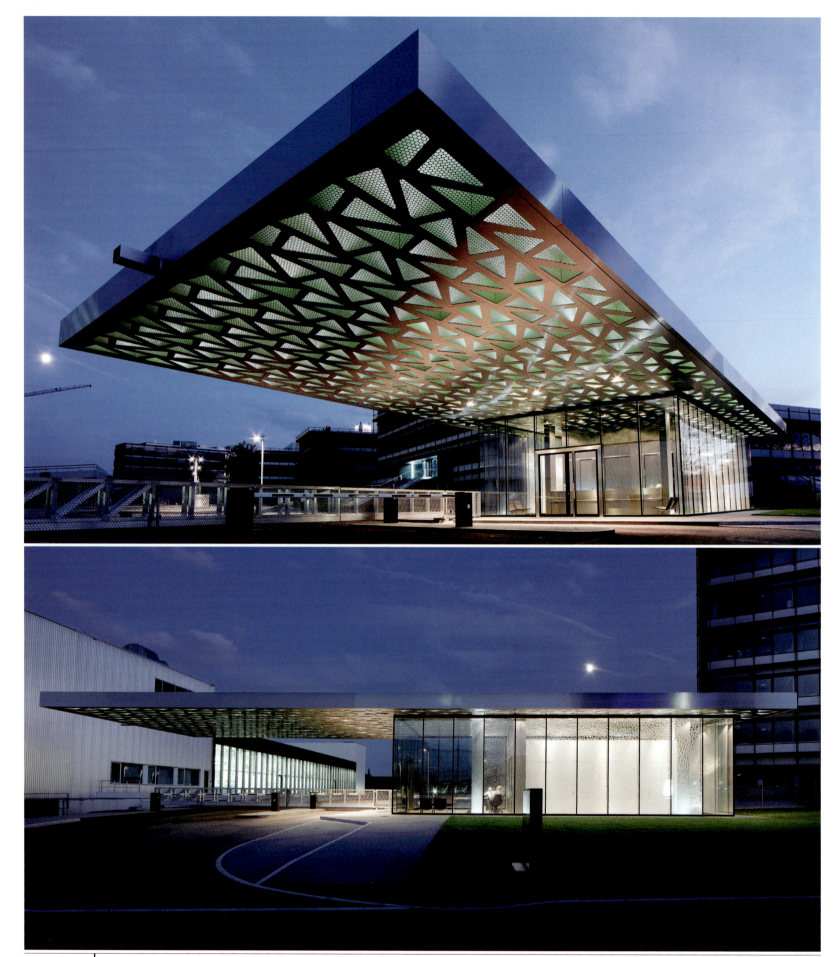

Barkow Leibinger Architekten
Gatehouse of Trumpf GmbH, Ditzingen, 2007
External views

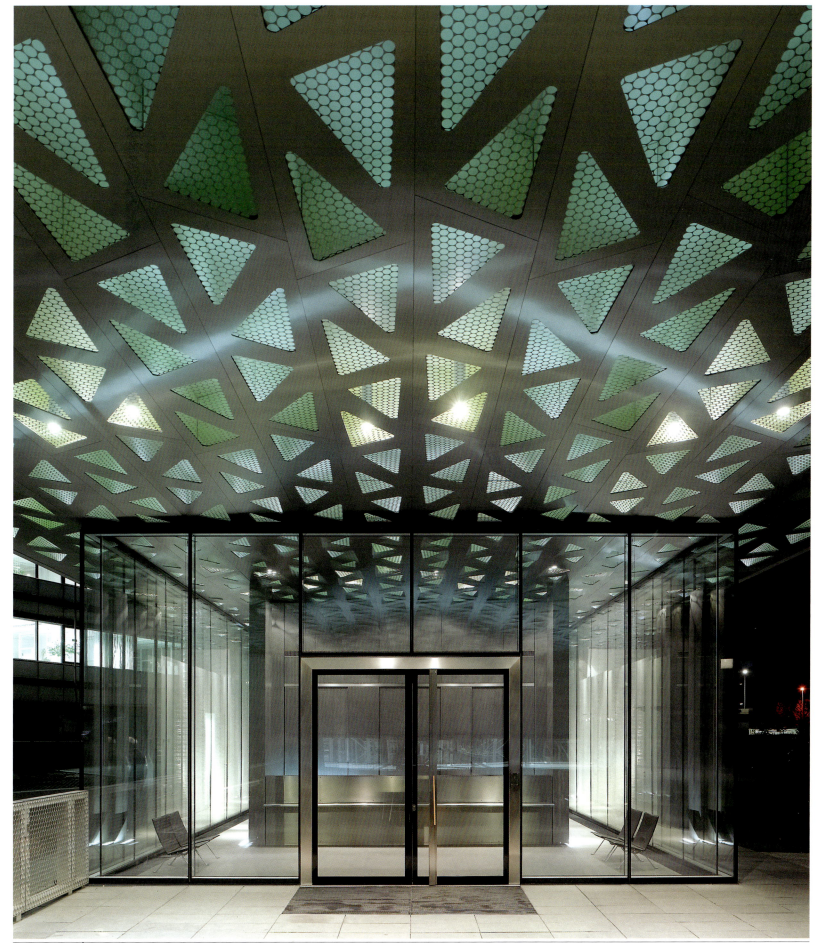

43 **Barkow Leibinger Architekten**
Gatehouse of Trumpf GmbH, Ditzingen, 2007
View of the honeycomb roof structure

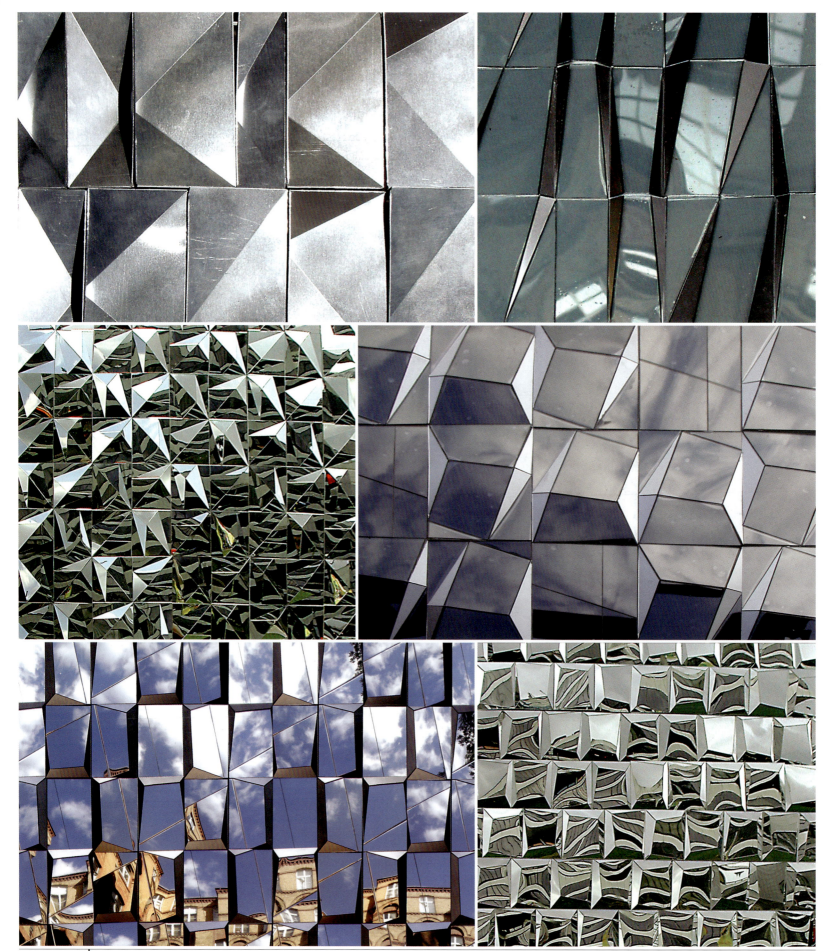

44   **Barkow Leibinger Architekten**
Trutec Building, Seoul, 2006
Façade studies for the Trutec office building

45 | **Barkow Leibinger Architekten**
Trutec Building, Seoul, 2006
External view of the fragmented mirror façade

46 **David Best**
Temple of Honor, Black Rock City, Burning Man 2003
Detail of the Temple of Honor at construction stage

48 **Max Bill**

variation 1

From: quinze variations sur un même thème, 1935–38, 1. reihe
Lithographic print and letterpress, 30 x 32 cm each
Max, Binia + Jakob Bill Foundation, Zurich
© 2008, ProLitteris, Zurich

variation 3

From: quinze variations sur un même thème, 1935–38, 1. reihe
Lithographic print and letterpress, 30 x 32 cm each
Max, Binia + Jakob Bill Foundation, Zurich
© 2008, ProLitteris, Zurich

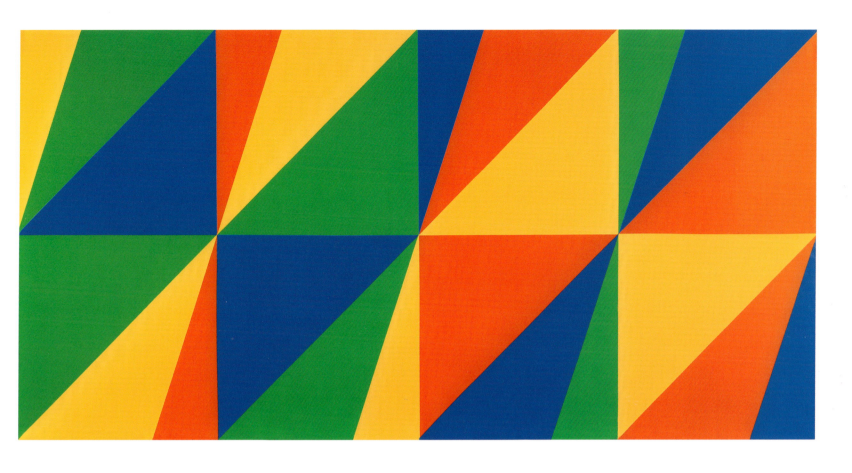

49

Max Bill
vier quantengleiche farben in acht gleichen feldern, 1973

Oil on canvas, 180 x 90 cm
Max, Binia + Jakob Bill Foundation, Zurich
© 2008, ProLitteris, Zurich

XVIII/XLIV

bill
79

Max Bill
vierfarbiger rhythmus, 1979

Silkscreen, 78 x 61 cm
Deutsche Bank Collection (Inv. no. K19840129)
© 2008, ProLitteris, Zurich

51   **Max Bill**
      dreieck

      From: 3 gleiche farbquanten (quadrat, dreieck, kreis), 1983. 11. reihe
      Silkscreen, series of 3 sheets, 70 x 70 cm
      Deutsche Bank Collection (Inv. no. K19840053)
      © 2008, ProLitteris, Zurich

Matthias Bitzer

The Deconstruction of Determination, 2007

Acrylic and lacquer on raw canvas, 196 x 165 cm (framed)
Courtesy of Galerie Iris Kadel, Karlsruhe

Matthias Bitzer
The Healer, 2007
Acrylic and ink on canvas, 190 x 160 cm
Courtesy of Galerie Iris Kadel, Karlsruhe

Matthias Bitzer
Fräulein Demimonde, 2007
Acrylic and ink on raw canvas, 250 x 190 cm
Courtesy of Galerie Iris Kadel, Karlsruhe

55 **Matthias Bitzer**
The Restless, 2007
Acrylic and ink on raw canvas, 250 x 200 cm
Courtesy of Galerie Iris Kadel, Karlsruhe

Blocher Blocher Partners
Engelhorn acc/es, Mannheim, 2007
External view of the wedge-shaped windows of the Engelhorn department store

Blocher Blocher Partners
Engelhorn acc/es, Mannheim, 2007
Detail of the façade

Tord Boontje
Watercolor, 2004
Digital print on silk
Studio Tord Boontje

Tord Boontje
Watercolor, 2004
Digital print on silk
Studio Tord Boontje

Chris Bosse
Digital Origami, 2007
In cooperation with students of the University of Technology, Sydney
Interior view of the origami installation, 72 Erskine, Sidney

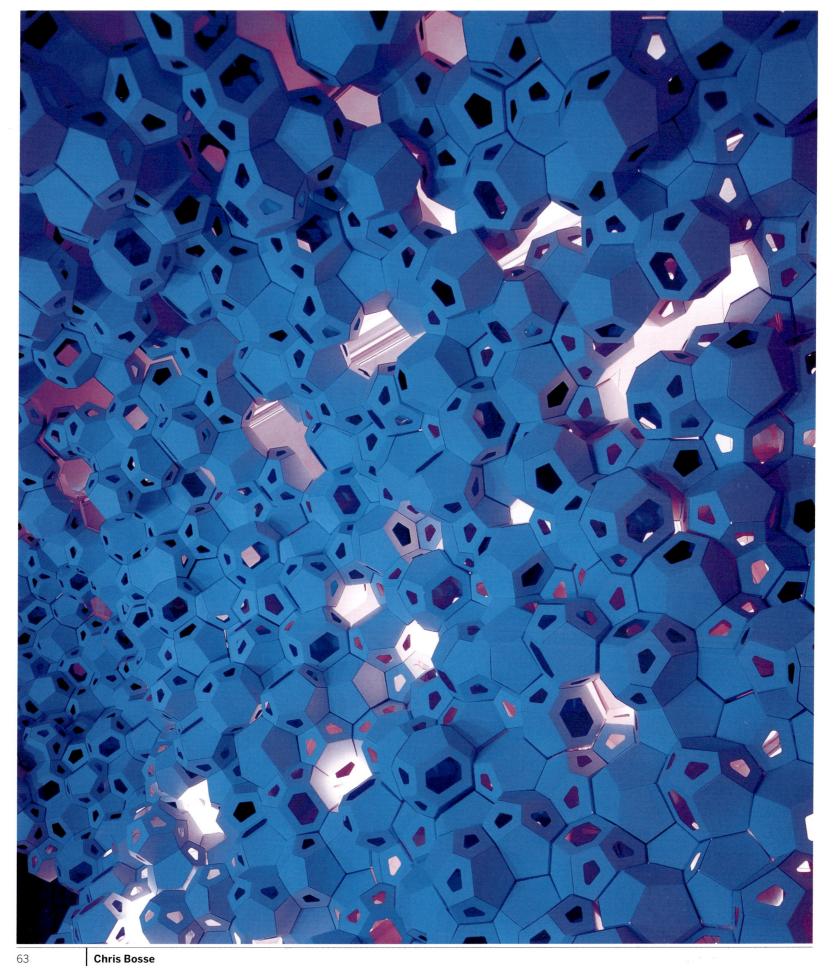

63 **Chris Bosse**
Digital Origami, 2007
In cooperation with students of the University of Technology, Sydney
Detail of cardboard modules

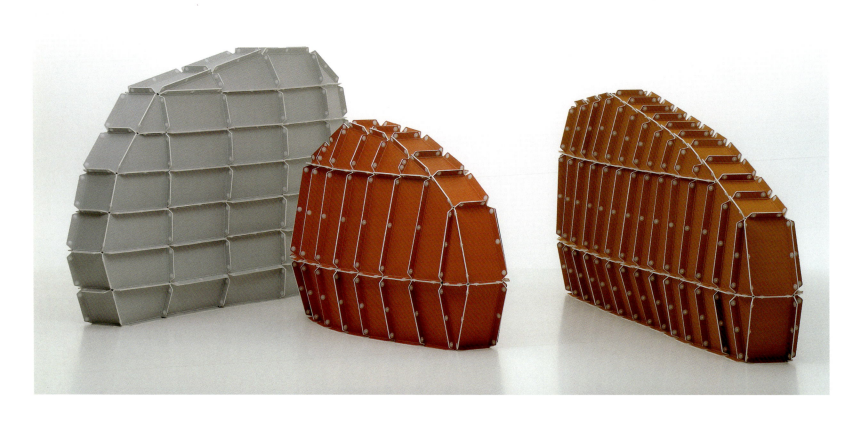

Ronan and Erwan Bouroullec
Roc, 2006
Partition walls made of cardboard modules
Manufacturer: Vitra

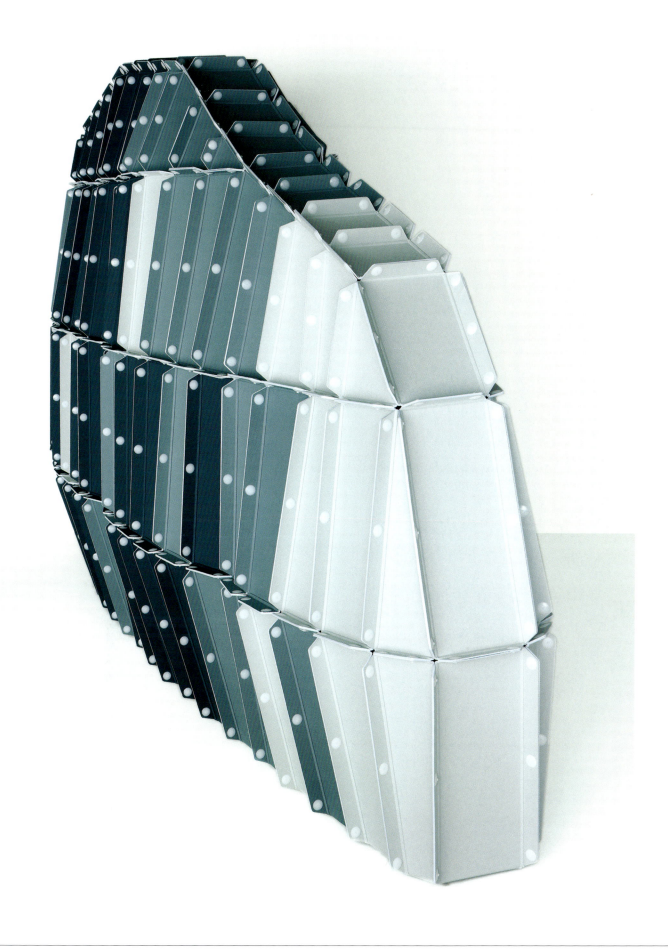

Ronan and Erwan Bouroullec
North Tiles, 2006
Assembling system made of textile modules
above: Detail of a textile wall
below: Interior view of the Kvadrat showroom, Stockholm
Manufacturer: Kvadrat

67 **Ronan and Erwan Bouroullec**
North Tiles, 2006
Assembling system made of textile modules
Interior views of the Kvadrat showroom, Stockholm
Manufacturer: Kvadrat

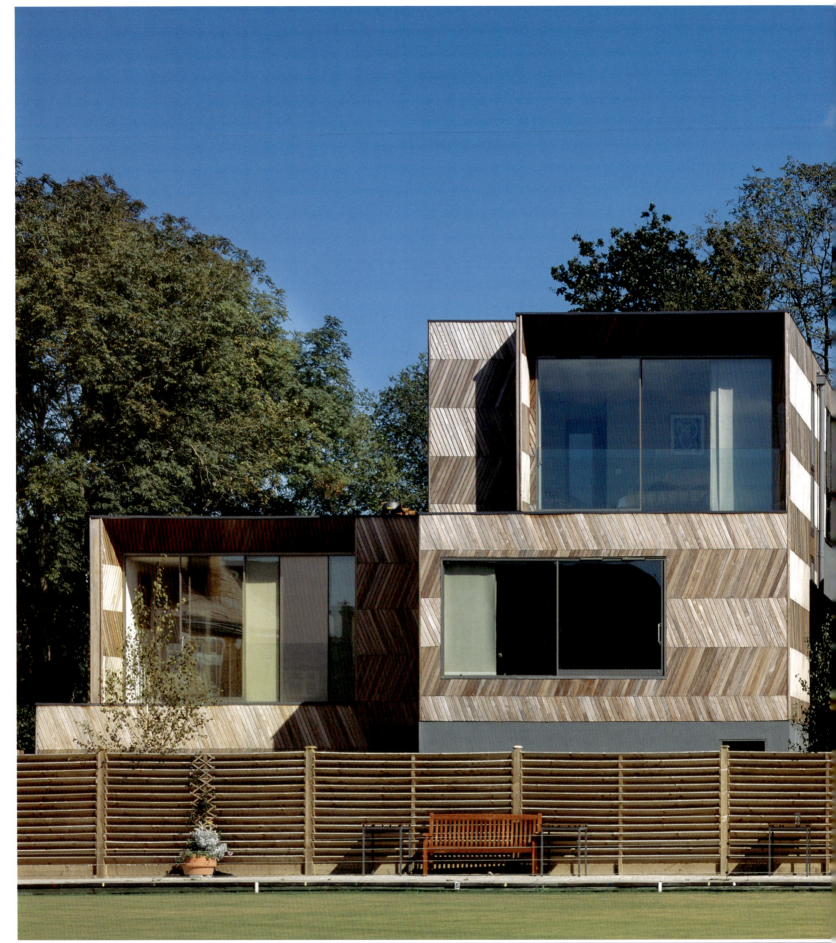

Alison Brooks Architects
Herringbone Houses, London, 2006
External view

Alison Brooks Architects

Herringbone Houses, London, 2006

The herringbone timber extends from the façade to the fences.

Alison Brooks Architects

Herringbone Houses, London, 2006

above: View from the garden
below: Details of the timber cladding

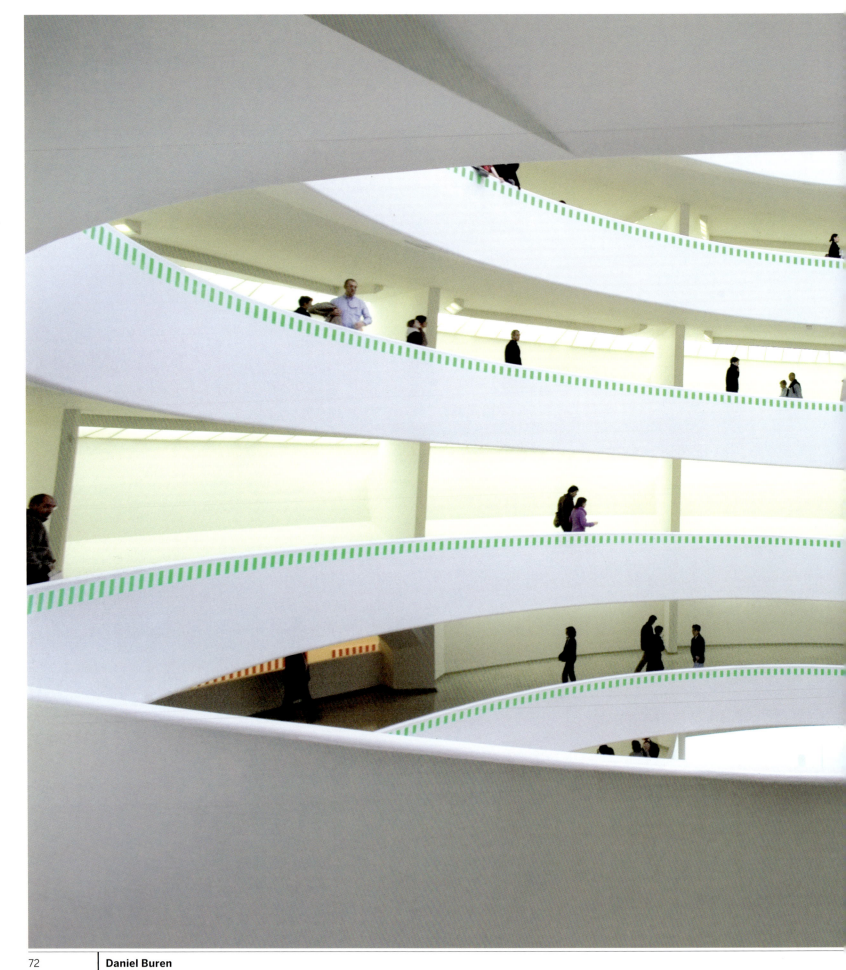

Daniel Buren
The Eye of the Storm: Works in situ by Daniel Buren,
Solomon R. Guggenheim Museum, New York,
March 25–June 8, 2005
Installation view
The Solomon R. Guggenheim Foundation, New York

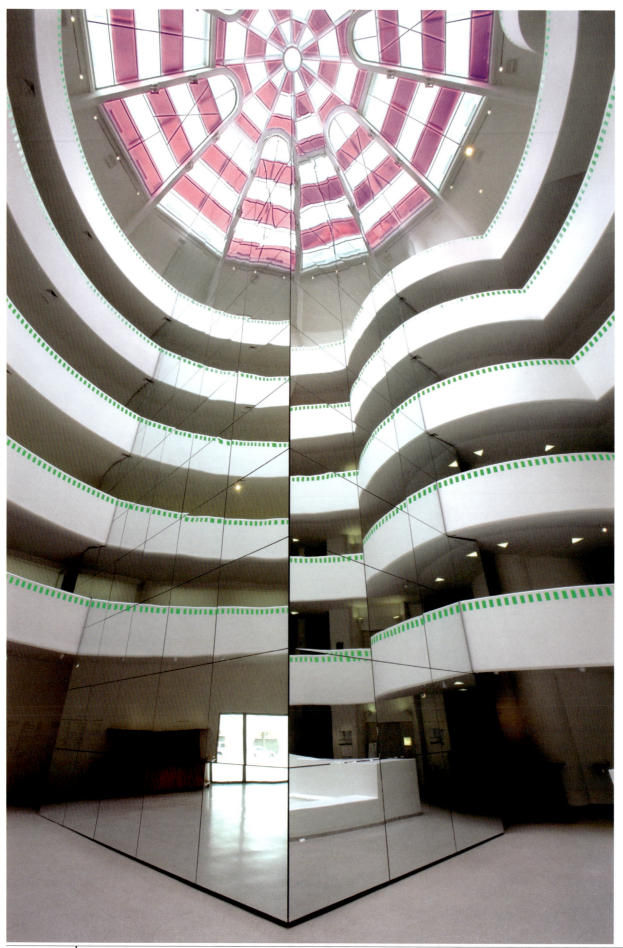

Daniel Buren
The Eye of the Storm: Works in situ by Daniel Buren,
Solomon R. Guggenheim Museum, New York,
March 25–June 8, 2005
Installation view
The Solomon R. Guggenheim Foundation, New York

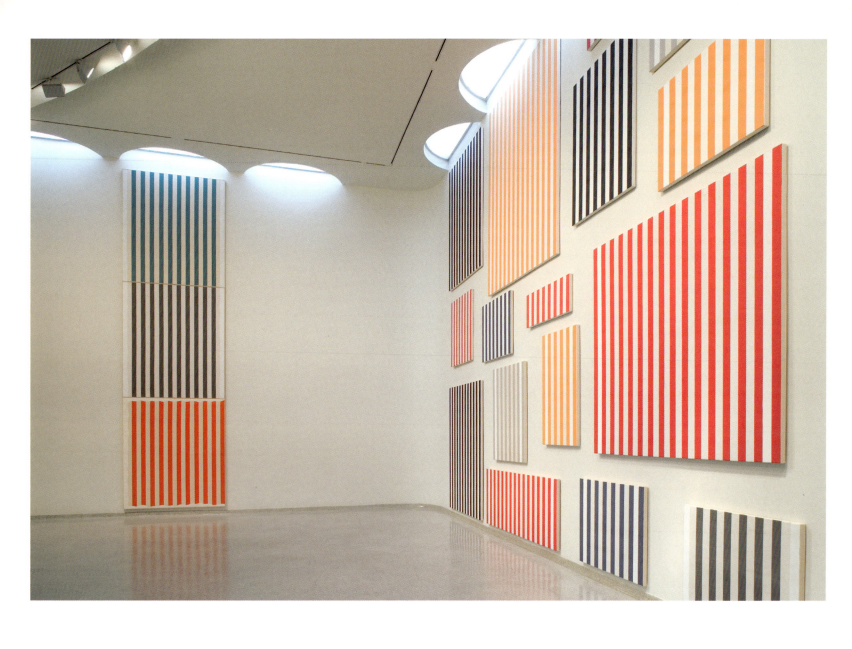

Daniel Buren
The Eye of the Storm: Works in situ by Daniel Buren,
Solomon R. Guggenheim Museum, New York,
March 25–June 8, 2005
Installation view
The Solomon R. Guggenheim Foundation, New York

Sun Young Byun
the house in the painting the painting in the house, 2007
Acrylic on canvas, 120 x 85 cm
Courtesy of Alexander Ochs Galleries Berlin/Beijing

Sun Young Byun

the house in the painting the painting in the house, 2007

Acrylic on canvas, 120 x 85 cm
Courtesy of Alexander Ochs Galleries Berlin/Beijing

c.neeon
Autumn/Winter 07/08 Collection "Sharing Secrets"

c.neeon
Autumn/Winter 07/08 Collection "Sharing Secrets"

84

Chalet 5
The Winner Takes it All, 2007

Groteske #02
Mixed media, 35.5 x 126.5 x 65.5 cm
Object view
Courtesy of Chalet 5, Zurich

Chalet 5
Come Out to Show, 2007
Groteske #01
Mixed media, wall painting, 112 x 200 x 56 cm
View of installation
Courtesy of Chalet 5, Zurich

Chalet 5

Smells like Victory, 2007

Groteske #07
Mixed media, wall painting, 120 x 237.5 x 73 cm
View of installation
Courtesy of Chalet 5, Zurich

Bjorn Copeland
Flat Leak Potential, 2007
Gel pen and mixed media on paper, 94 x 124 cm (framed)
Courtesy of the artist and China Art Objects Gallery, Los Angeles

Bjorn Copeland
Cover Potential, 2007
Mixed media on paper, 76.1 x 76.2 cm
Courtesy of the artist and China Art Objects Gallery, Los Angeles

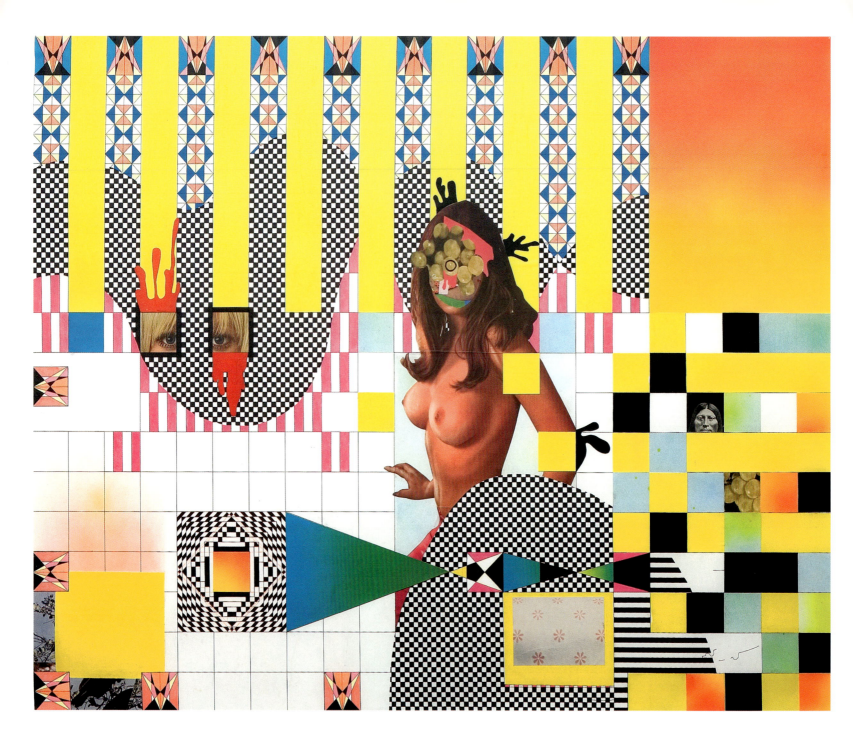

Bjorn Copeland
Money Shot, 2006

Gel pen and mixed media on paper, 94 x 124 cm
Courtesy of the artist and China Art Objects Gallery, Los Angeles

Bjorn Copeland
Vertical Change, 2007

Gel pen and mixed media on paper, 124 x 94 cm
Courtesy of the artist and China Art Objects Gallery, Los Angeles

Mia Cullin
Flake, 2007
Tyvek modules
Manufacturer: Woodnotes

Jacob Dahlgren

I, the world, things, life, 2007

The Nordic Pavilion, Venice Biennale 2007
Interactive dart board installation, 1517 x 396 cm

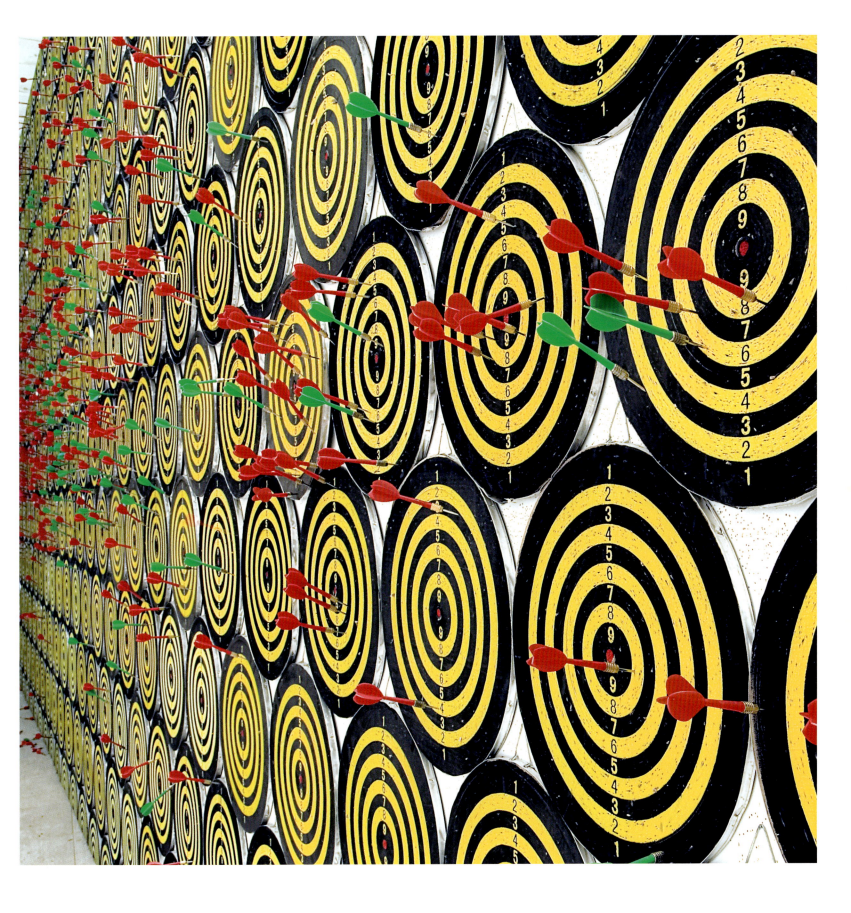

95 **Jacob Dahlgren**

I, the world, things, life, 2007

The Nordic Pavilion, Venice Biennale 2007
Interactive dart board installation, 1517 x 396 cm
Detail

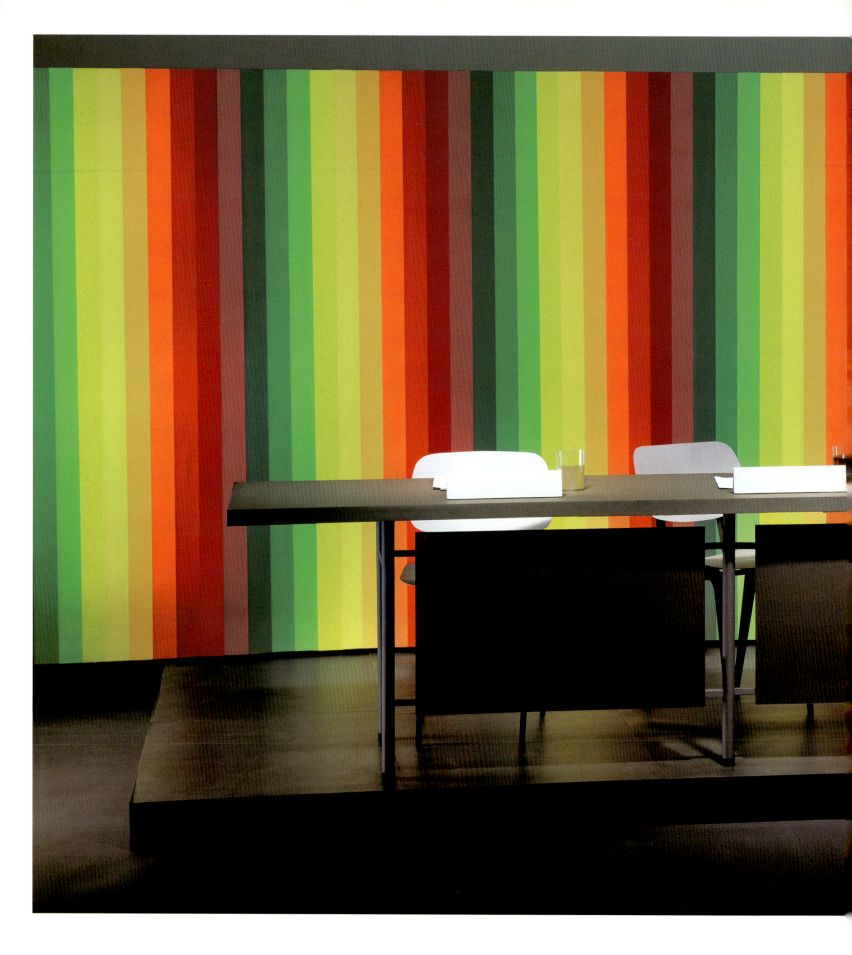

Thomas Demand

Studio, 1997

C-Print/Diasec, 183.5 x 349.5 cm
Courtesy of Monika Sprüth/Philomene Magers, Cologne Munich London
© 2008, ProLitteris, Zurich

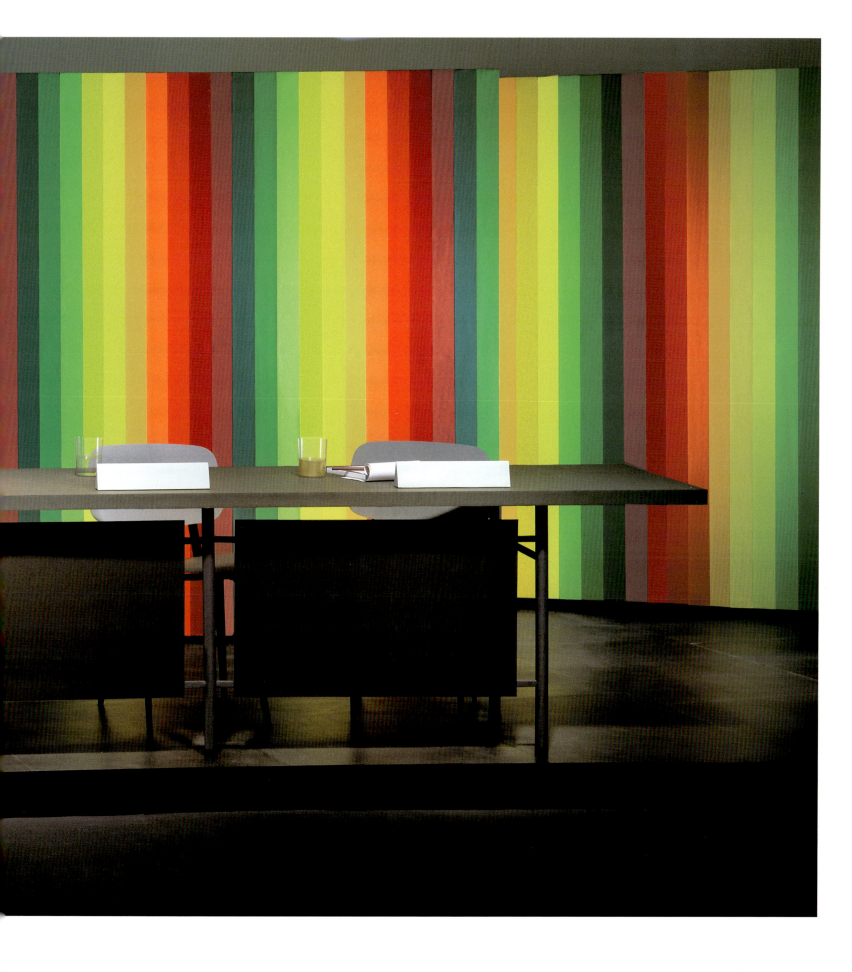

Thomas Demand
Efeu, 2006
Wallpaper
Detail
Courtesy of Monika Sprüth/Philomene Magers, Cologne Munich London
© 2008, ProLitteris, Zurich

Thomas Demand
Efeu, 2006
Wallpaper
View of installation, Serpentine Gallery, 2006
Courtesy of Monika Sprüth/Philomene Magers, Cologne Munich London

Thomas Demand

Fassade, 2004

Offset print on affiche paper, 300 x 1250 cm
View of installation, Kunsthaus Bregenz, 2004
Courtesy of Monika Sprüth/Philomene Magers, Cologne Munich London

Thomas Demand

Fassade, 2004

Offset print on affiche paper, 300 x 1250 cm
Detail
Courtesy of Monika Sprüth/Philomene Magers, Cologne Munich London
© 2008, ProLitteris, Zurich

Liz Deschenes
Moiré #9, 2007
UV laminated C-Print, 152.4 x 116.8 cm (framed)
Unique print
Courtesy of Sutton Lane, London

103 | **Liz Deschenes**
Moiré #10, 2007
UV laminated C-Print, 152.4 x 116.8 cm (framed)
Unique print
Courtesy of Sutton Lane, London

Liz Deschenes
Moiré #11, 2007
UV laminated C-print, 152.4 x 116.8 cm (framed)
Unique print
Courtesy of Sutton Lane, London

Liz Deschenes
Moiré #12, 2007
UV laminated C-Print, 152.4 x 116.8 cm (framed)
Unique print
Courtesy of Sutton Lane, London

Liz Deschenes
Moiré #13, 2007
UV laminated C-Print, 152.4 x 116.8 cm (framed)
Unique print
Courtesy of Sutton Lane, London

Liz Deschenes
Moiré #14, 2007
UV laminated C-Print, 152.4 x 116.8 cm (framed)
Unique print
Courtesy of Sutton Lane, London

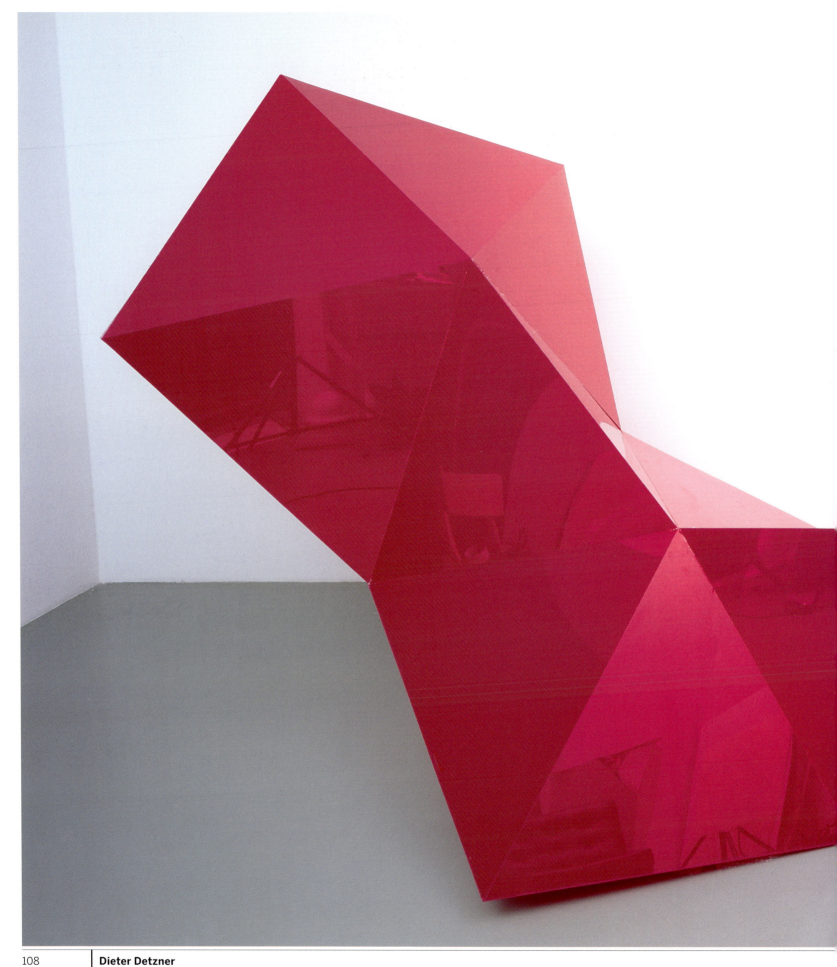

Dieter Detzner
André, 2007
Perspex, 177.6 x 325.7 x 85.3 cm
Courtesy of Studio Sassa Trülzsch, Berlin

Dieter Detzner
Gabriele, 2007
Perspex, 95 x 105 x 20 cm
Private collection
Courtesy of Studio Sassa Trülzsch, Berlin

111 **Dieter Detzner**
Robert, 2006

Perspex, 90 x 160 x 160 cm
Private collection Alexander Lagemann
Courtesy of Studio Sassa Trülzsch, Berlin

Birgit Dieker
Olga, 2006/07
Clothing, h 189 cm

Birgit Dieker
La Vie en Rose (II), 2007
Clothing, 25 x 17 x 18.5 cm

Birgit Dieker
Efka, 2006
Clothing, 54 x 26 x 32 cm
Private collection Berlin

Birgit Dieker
Wirbel, 2002
Clothing, polystyrene, steel, h 640 cm

FAT

Sint Lucas Art Academy, Boxtel, The Netherlands, 2006

above: External view of the pre-cast concrete screens
below left: Doorway detail in the foyer
below right: Reception

FAT
Sint Lucas Art Academy, Boxtel, The Netherlands, 2006
External view of the pre-cast concrete frame at the front entrance

118   **Thom Faulders Architecture/Studio M**
Airspace Tokyo, 2007
Façade made of laser-cut aluminium and plastic composite sheets
Screen design: Thom Faulders in collaboration with Proces2, San Francisco
Building design: Hajime Masubuchi/Studio M, Tokyo
External view by night

Thom Faulders Architecture/Studio M
Airspace Tokyo, 2007
Façade made of laser-cut aluminium, plastic composite sheets
Screen design: Thom Faulders in collaboration with Proces2, San Francisco
Building design: Hajime Masubuchi/Studio M, Tokyo
Façade details

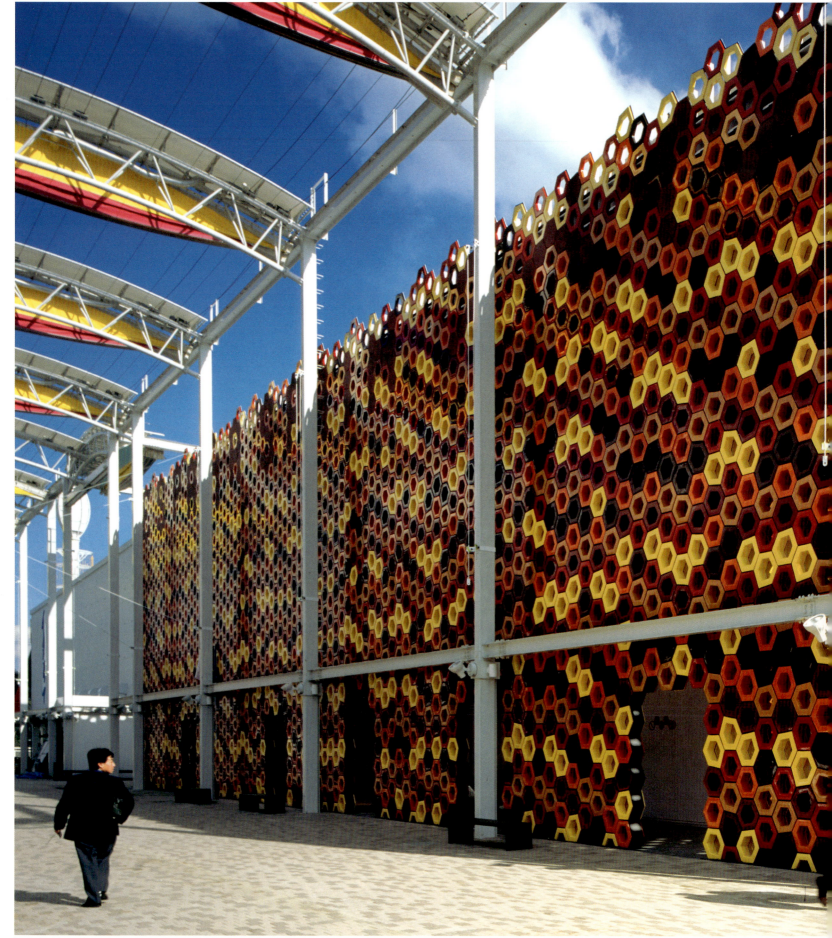

Foreign Office Architects
Spanish Pavilion, World Expo 2005, Aichi, Japan
External view

Foreign Office Architects
Spanish Pavilion, World Expo 2005, Aichi, Japan
Detail of the hexagonal ceramic modules

Foreign Office Architects
Spanish Pavilion, World Expo 2005, Aichi, Japan
View from a distance

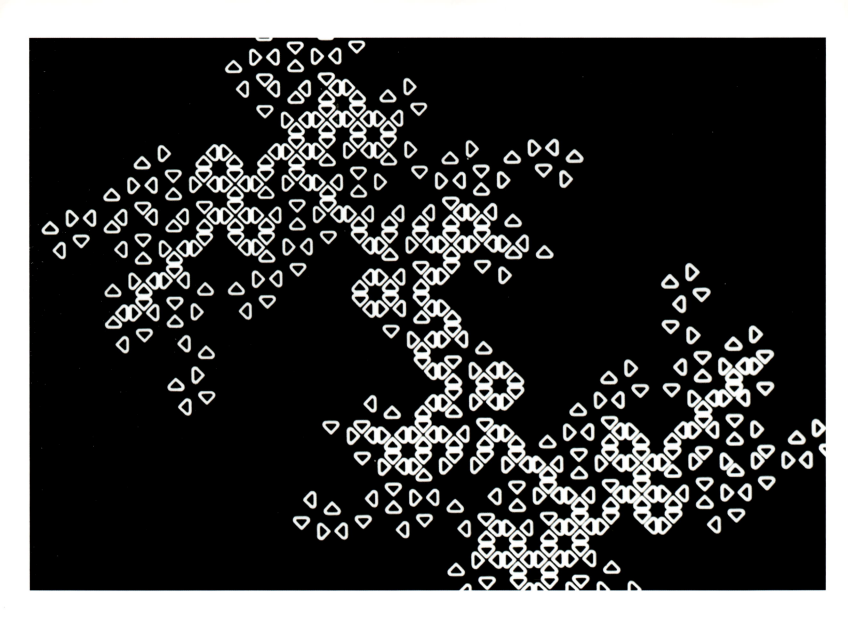

126 | **Herbert W. Franke**
From the Drakula series, 1970/71
Computer-generated plotter drawings

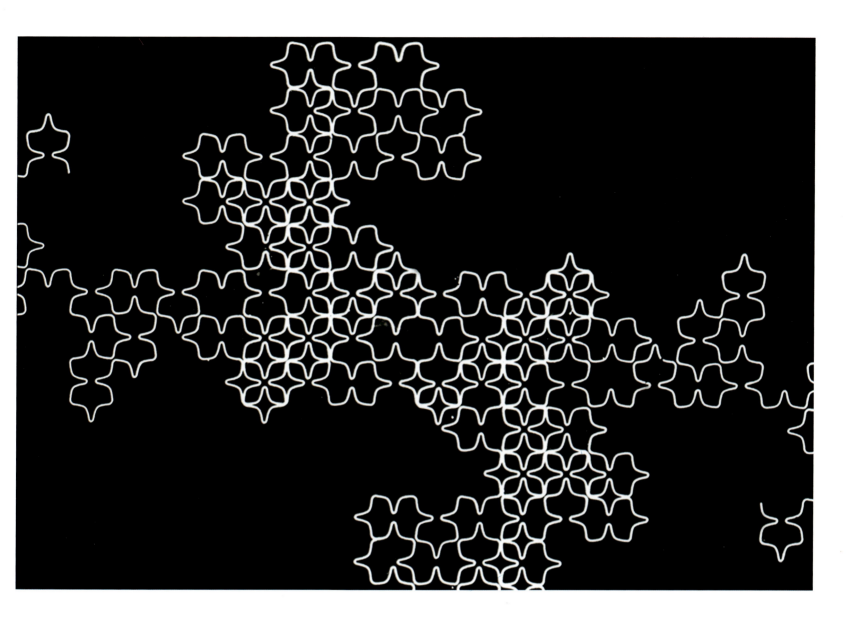

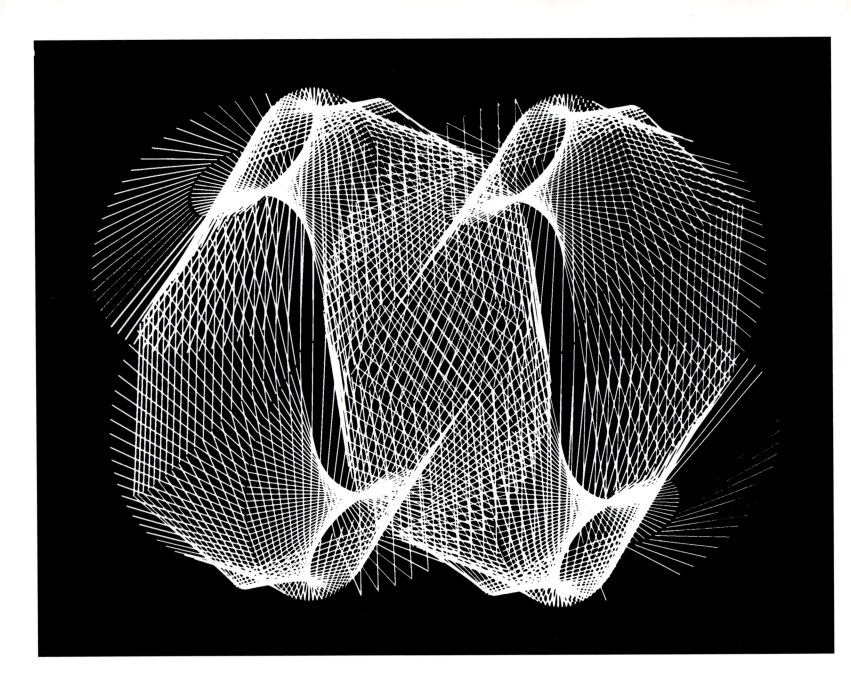

Herbert W. Franke

From the Rotations/Projections series, 1974

Computer-generated animation sequences (phase pictures)
Developed for the "Laser" ballet by Walter Haupt
Client: Experimental Stage, Bavarian State Opera Munich

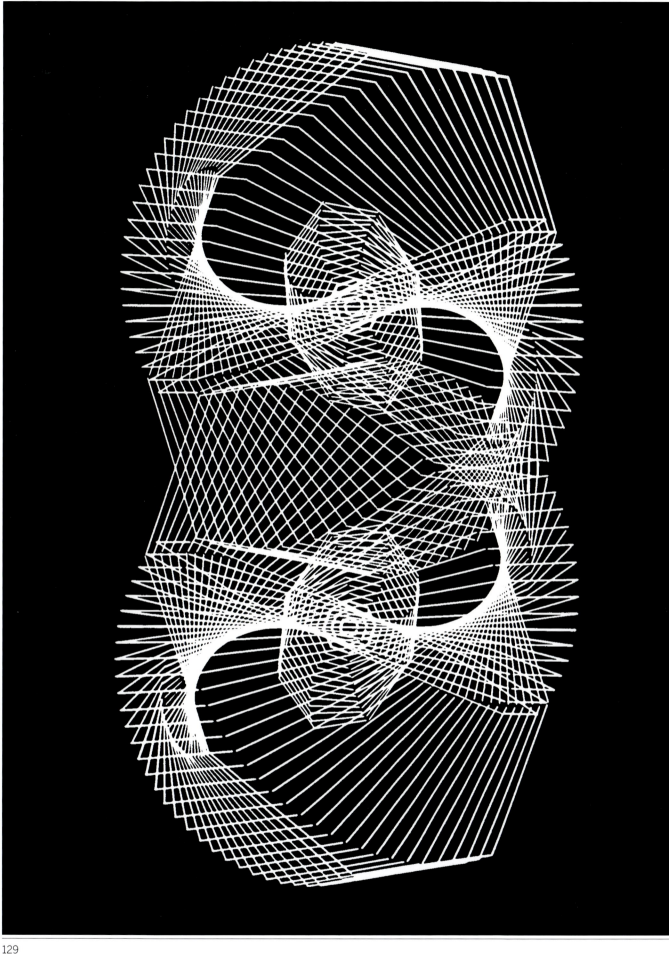

129

Herbert W. Franke

From the Mondrian series, 1980

Phase pictures from an interactively controllable operational sequence
with sound effects
Client: Texas Instruments

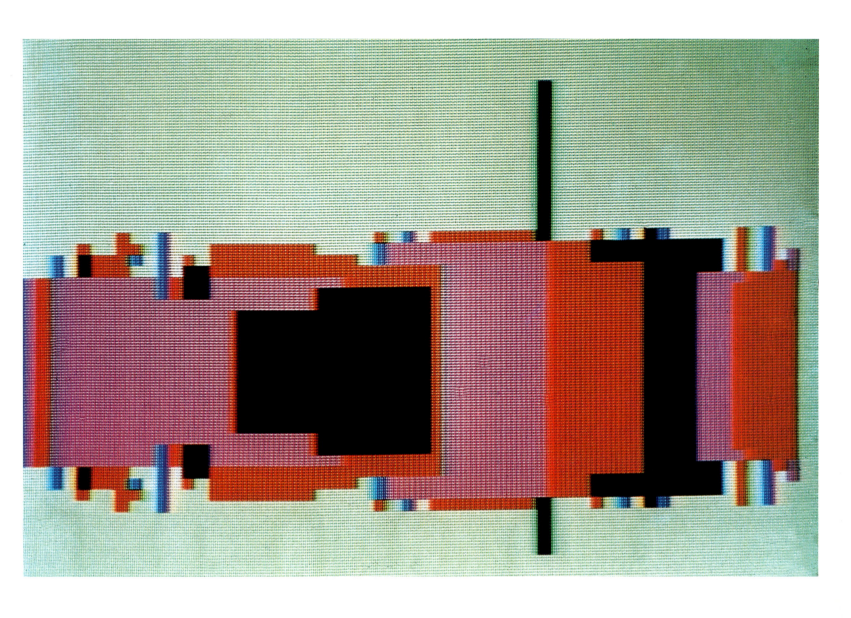

Richard Buckminster Fuller

Geodesic dome, US Pavilion, World Expo 1967, Montréal

Diameter: approx. 76 m
External view
Courtesy of The Estate of R. Buckminster Fuller

Richard Buckminster Fuller

Geodesic dome, US Pavilion, World Expo 1967, Montréal

Diameter: approx. 76 m
Inside of the dome
Courtesy of The Estate of R. Buckminster Fuller

134 **Richard Buckminster Fuller**
Geodesic dome, US Pavilion, World Expo 1967, Montréal
Diameter: approx. 76 m
Details of the dome structure
Courtesy of The Estate of R. Buckminster Fuller

136 **Diane von Furstenberg**
Spiral Hearts, 2003
Hand-knotted rug made from Tibetan wool, 274 x 183 cm
Manufacturer: The Rug Company

138   **Sarah van Gameren**
Burn Burn Burn, 2007
Performance with flammable paint
Before the performance

Sarah van Gameren
Burn Burn Burn, 2007
Performance with flammable paint
After the performance

140 **Poul Gernes**
Left-hand wall: Target paintings, 1966–76
Varnish on masonite, 122 x 122 cm each
Courtesy of Estate of Poul Gernes

Centre wall:
Stripe paintings, 1965
Varnish on masonite, 122 x 122 cm each
Courtesy of Estate of Poul Gernes

Right-hand wall:
Target paintings, 1970
Varnish on masonite, 85 x 85 cm each
Courtesy of Estate of Poul Gernes

Poul Gernes
Untitled, 1980

Varnish on masonite, 122 x 122 cm
12 parts
Courtesy of Estate of Poul Gernes

142 **Poul Gernes**
Wall with various works, 1960–65
Courtesy of Estate of Poul Gernes

143 **Poul Gernes**
Variations on the Danish flag, 1975
Varnish on masonite, 91 x 91 cm each
Courtesy of Estate of Poul Gernes

144

Henriette Grahnert

Ja gesagt, Oh nein gedacht, 2007

Oil on canvas, 220 x 170 cm
Courtesy of galerieKleindienst, Leipzig

Henriette Grahnert
nicht kompatibel, 2007
Oil on canvas, 180 x 150 cm
Courtesy of galerieKleindienst, Leipzig

146

Hervé Graumann

Oriental Carpet I, 2006

Endura print mounted on alu dibond, 180 x 258 cm
Courtesy of Galerie Guy Bärtschi, Geneva

Hervé Graumann
e-still life, 2006
Endura print mounted on alu dibond, 180 x 220 cm
Courtesy of Galerie Guy Bärtschi, Geneva

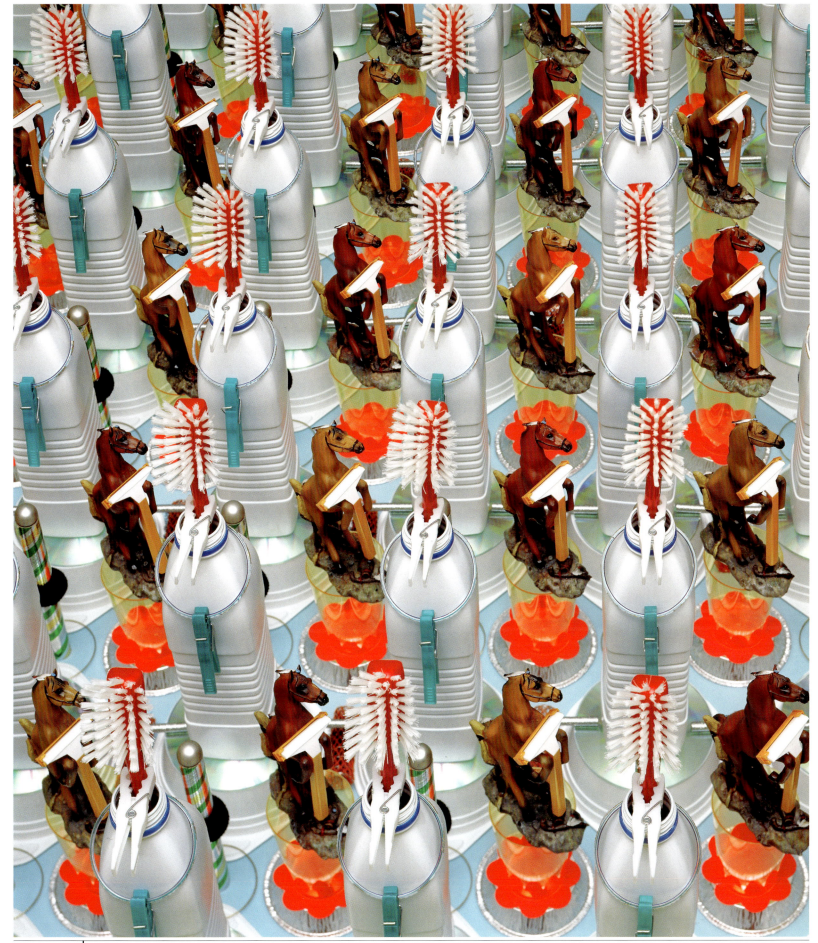

Hervé Graumann
Crazy Horse II, 2006
Endura print mounted on alu dibond, 180 x 220 cm
Courtesy of Galerie Guy Bärtschi, Geneva

Hervé Graumann
Vanité 2b, 2003
Ilfochrome mounted on aluminium, 116 x 186 cm
Courtesy of Galerie Guy Bärtschi, Geneva

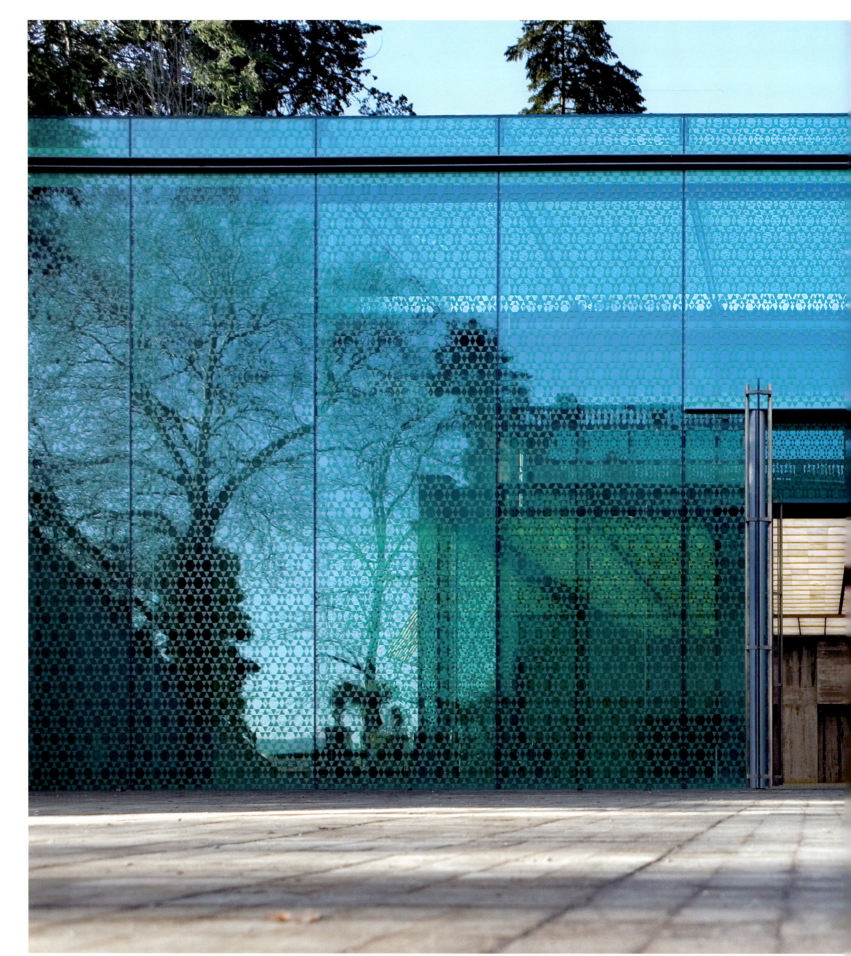

152   **Grazioli Krischanitz ARGE**
Extension of the Museum Rietberg, Zurich, 2007
The entrance pavilion with its green glass façade and its backlit onyx ceiling inside.

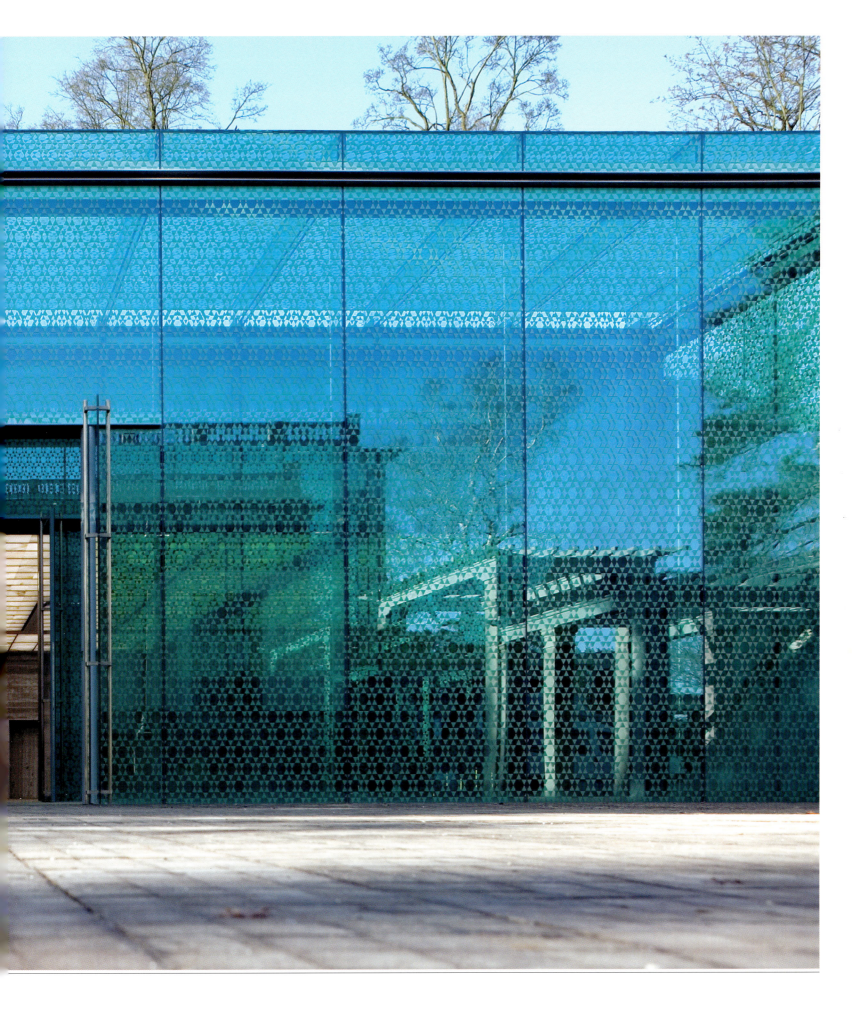

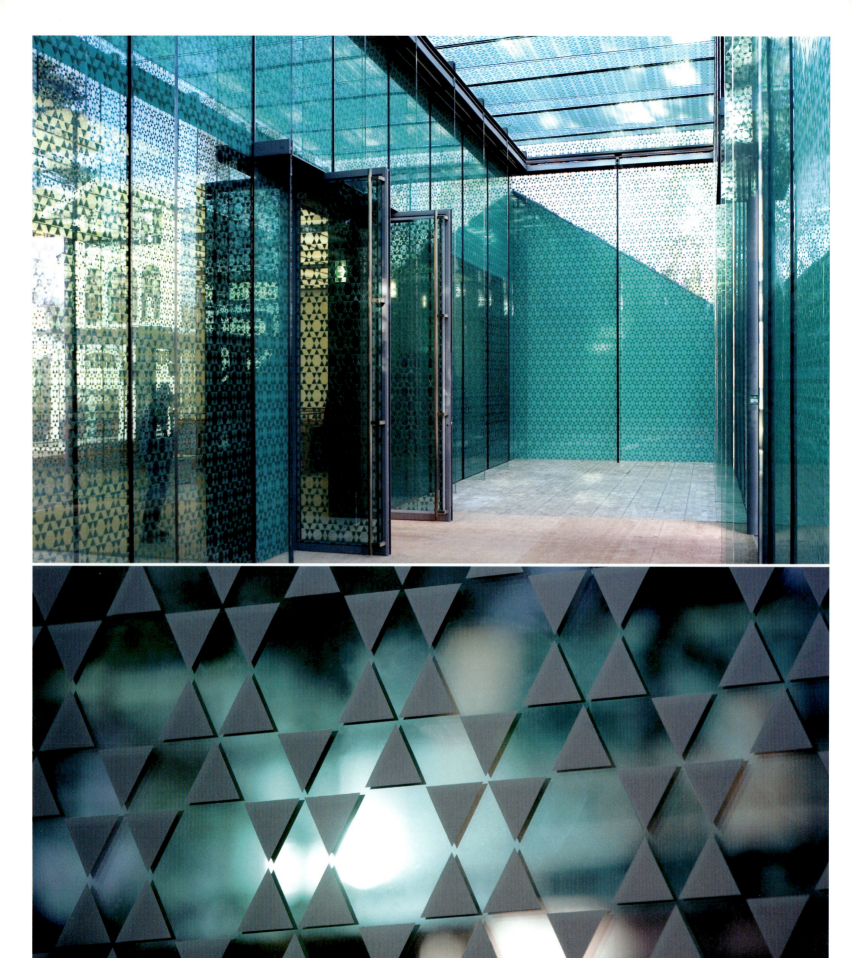

154   **Grazioli Krischanitz ARGE**
Extension of the Museum Rietberg, Zurich, 2007
above: Interior view of the pavilion
below: Detail of the patterned glass expanses

Grazioli Krischanitz ARGE
Extension of the Museum Rietberg, Zurich, 2007

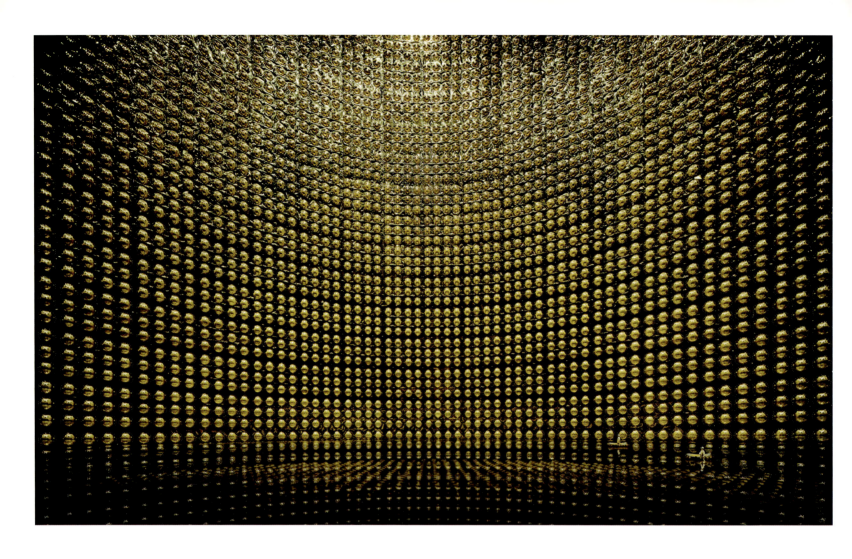

Andreas Gursky
Kamiokande, 2007
C-Print, 222 x 357 x 6.2 cm (framed)
Courtesy Monika Sprüth/Philomene Magers, Cologne Munich London
© Andreas Gursky/2008, ProLitteris, Zurich

157 | **Andreas Gursky**
Kathedrale I, 2007
C-Print, 237 x 333 x 6.2 cm (framed)
Courtesy Monika Sprüth/Philomene Magers, Cologne Munich London
© Andreas Gursky/2008, ProLitteris, Zurich

158 **Susanne Happle**
Solid Poetry, 2006
Concrete tiles
Manufacturer: Frederik Molenschot

Heatherwick Studio
Boiler Suit, Guy's and St. Thomas' Hospital, London, 2007
Panels made of stainless steel braid

Heatherwick Studio

Boiler Suit, Guy's and St. Thomas' Hospital, London, 2007

Panels made of stainless steel braid
above: Exterior day time view
below: The hospital boiler-room seen from outside at dusk

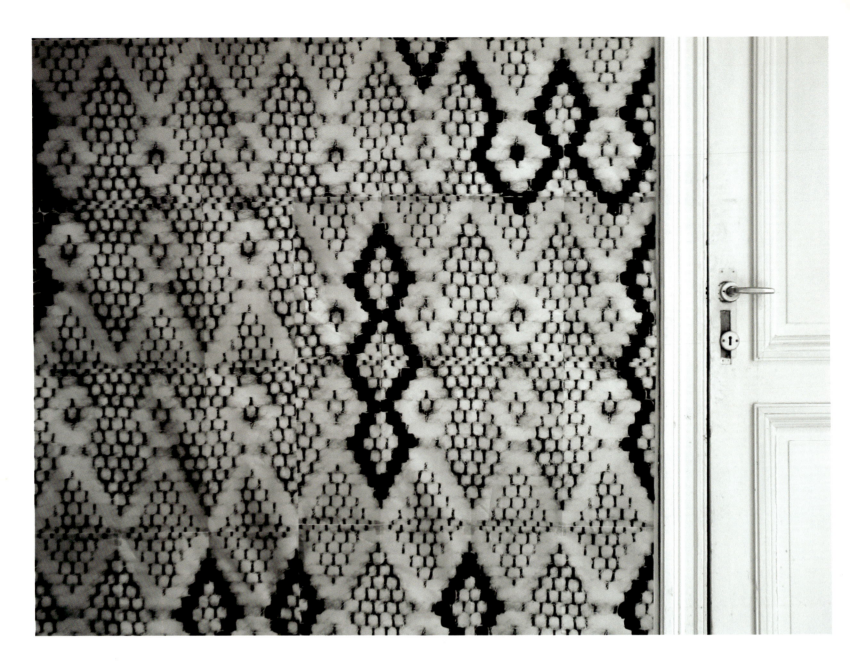

162 **Britt Helbig**
Wall To Wall, 2006
Wallpaper modules, photography
Detail

Britt Helbig
Wall To Wall, 2006
Wallpaper modules, photography
View of installation

164 **Matthias Hoch**
Brüssel #8, 2001

C-Print, 150 x 191 cm
Courtesy of Dogenhaus Galerie Leipzig
© 2008, ProLitteris, Zurich

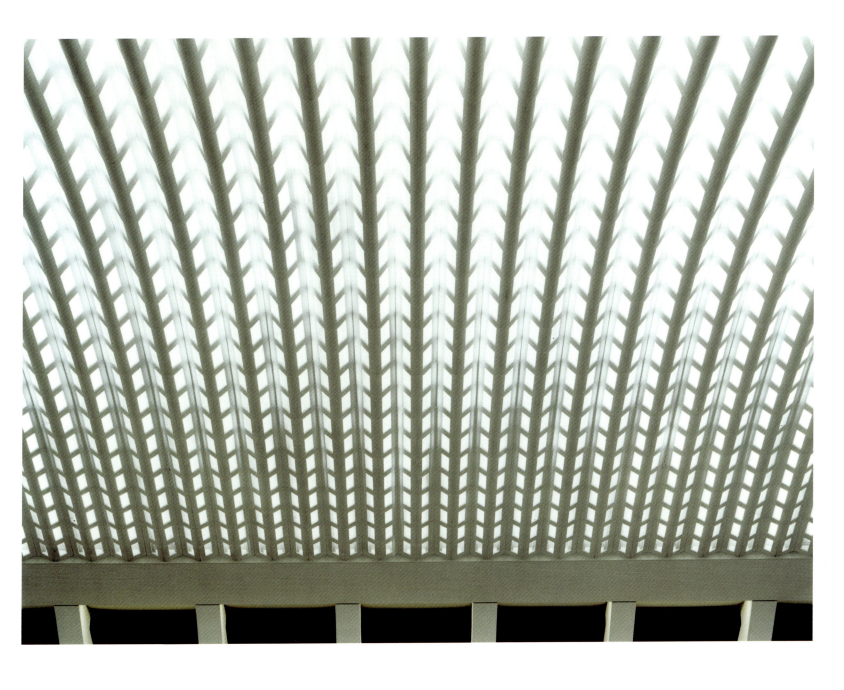

Matthias Hoch
Vatikan #26, 2004

C-Print, 178 x 227 cm
Courtesy of Dogenhaus Galerie Leipzig
© 2008, ProLitteris, Zurich

166 **Matthias Hoch**
Amsterdam #15, 2002

C-Print, 80 x 108 cm
Courtesy of Dogenhaus Galerie Leipzig
© 2008, ProLitteris, Zurich

167 | **Matthias Hoch**
Brüssel #2, 2001

C-Print, 180 x 151 cm
Courtesy of Dogenhaus Galerie Leipzig
© 2008, ProLitteris, Zurich

168 **Josef Hoffmann**

Pattern, without year

Pencil, black ink on paper, 29.8 x 40.8 cm
Collections of the University of Applied Arts, Vienna
(Inv. no. 27)

169 **Josef Hoffmann**
Geometric abstraction, about 1925
Ink on paper, 29.5 x 29.5 cm
Collection J. Hummel, Vienna

170   **Josef Hoffmann**
       Elis Z72, 1925–30

       Fabric design
       Pencil, black ink on board, 24.5 x 20.9 cm
       MAK–Austrian Museum of Applied Arts/Contemporary Art, Vienna

171   **Josef Hoffmann**
        Elis Z73, 1925–30
        Fabric design
        Pencil, black ink on board, 16.2 x 14.2 cm
        MAK – Austrian Museum of Applied Arts/Contemporary Art, Vienna

172 | **Jim Isermann**
Untitled (0107), 2007;
Vega (0699), 1999;
Untitled (0300), 2000
View of installation "Vinyl Smash Up 1999–2007", Deitch Projects, New York

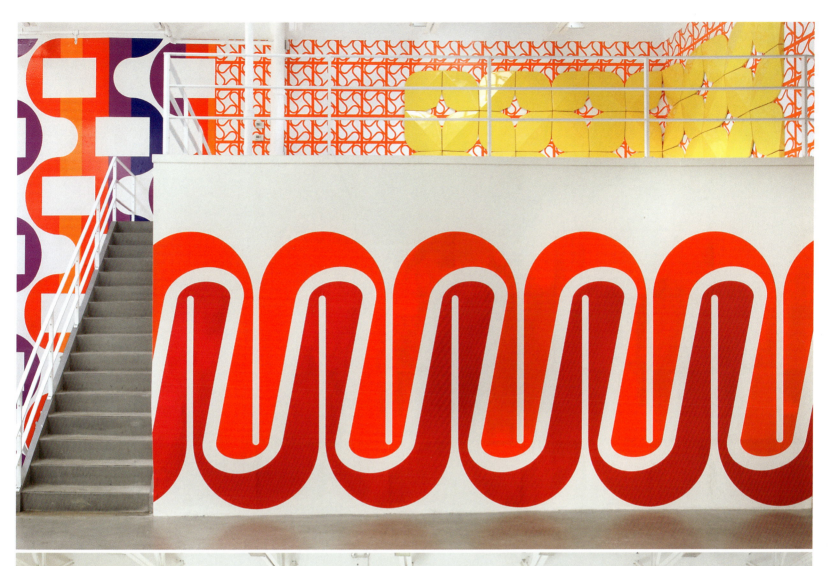

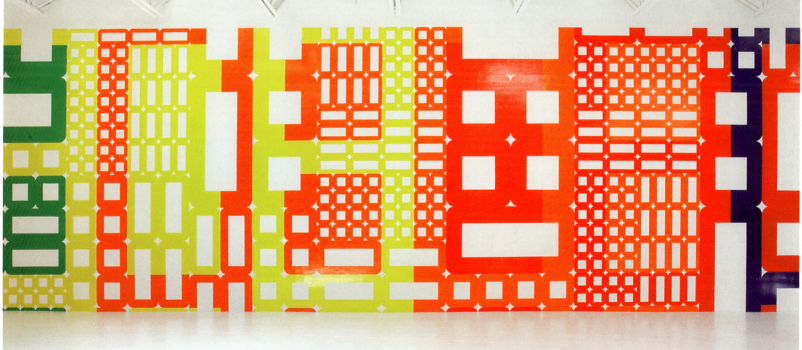

173   **Jim Isermann**
Untitled (0700), 2000
Views of installation "Vinyl Smash Up 1999–2007", Deitch Projects, New York

below:
Vega (0699), 1999
Views of installation "Vinyl Smash Up 1999–2007", Deitch Projects, New York

174 **Jim Isermann**
Portikus, Untitled (0900), 2000
Thermal die-cut vinyl, plotter-cut mylar decals,
overall approximately 488 cm x 732 x 1580 cm
Installation: Portikus, Frankfurt am Main

Kapitza
Graphic Pattern, 2008
Pattern font

Kapitza
Graphic Pattern, 2008
Pattern font

180 **Klein Dytham Architecture**

Heidi House, Tokyo, 2005

Glass, plywood

above: Exterior view of the glass-encased wooden façade

below: Details of the window openings and doorknobs

181 **Klein Dytham Architecture**
Heidi House, Tokyo, 2005
Glass, plywood
View of the interior

Klein Dytham Architecture
R3 Ukishima/Aicafe54, Naha, Okinawa, Japan 2007
Façade screen made of perforated concrete
External view of street front at night

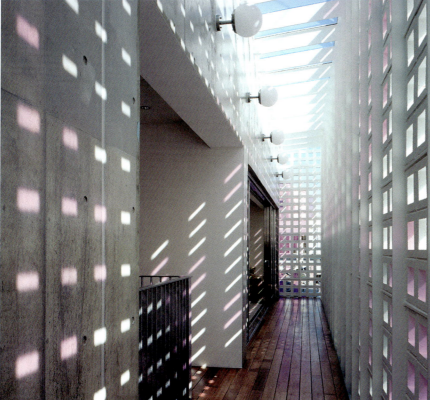

Klein Dytham Architecture

R3 Ukishima/Aicafe54, Okinawa, Japan 2007

Façade screen made of perforated concrete
above: View of the screen and its pixelated pink orchid pattern
below: Internal views (the cafe on the right)

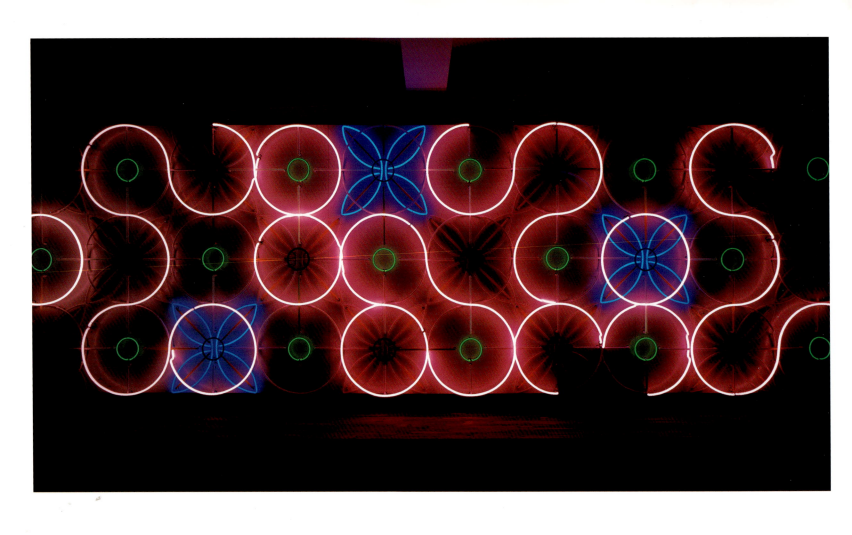

184 | **Astrid Krogh**
Polytics, 2003
Neon wallpaper, 256 neon tubes, 250 x 720 cm
Client: The Danish Parliament

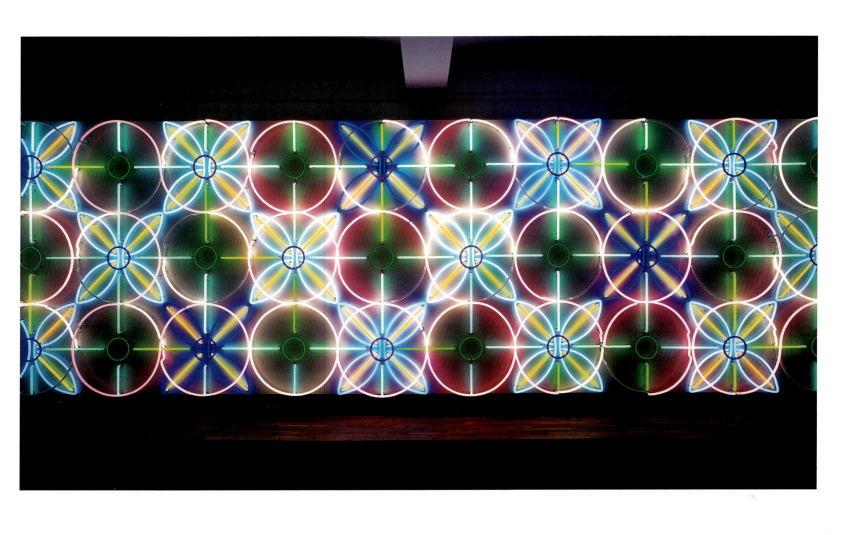

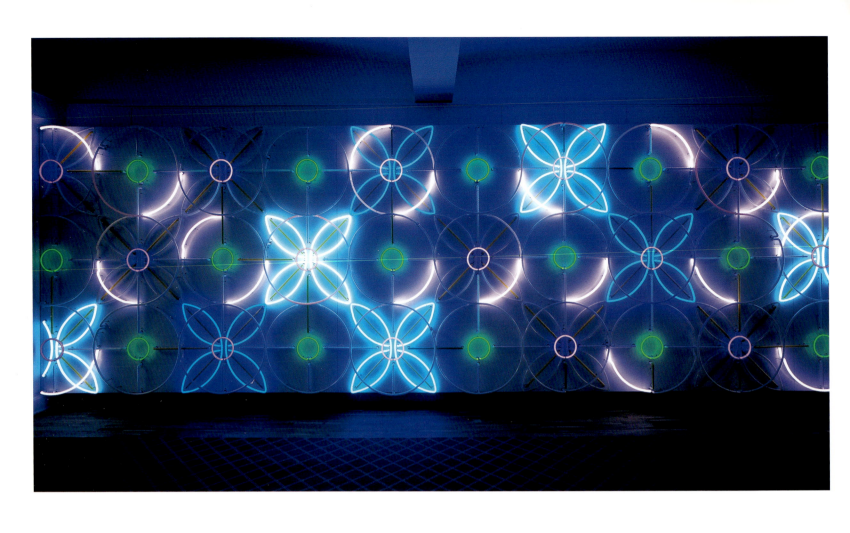

Astrid Krogh

Polytics, 2003

Neon wallpaper, 256 neon tubes, 250 x 720 cm
Client: The Danish Parliament

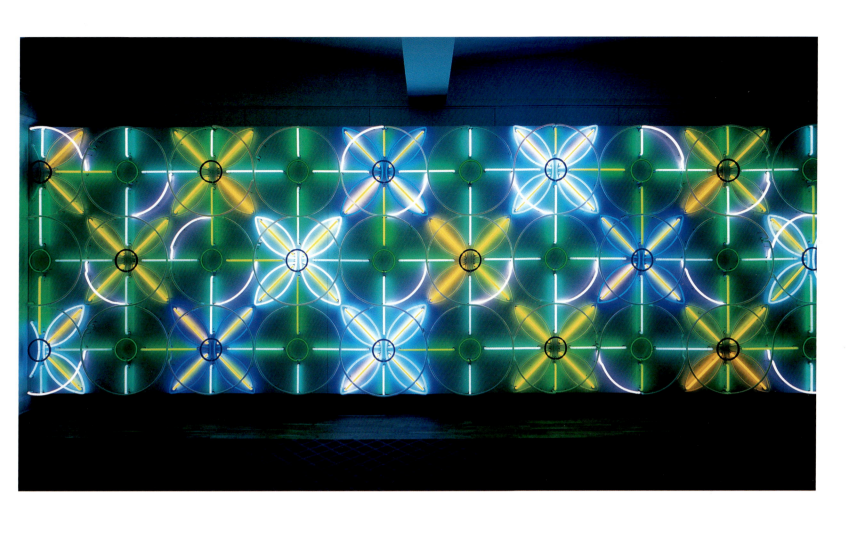

Kengo Kuma
Teahouse, 2007
Museum of Applied Arts, Frankfurt/Main
Interior view of the inflated structure

189 **Kengo Kuma**
Teahouse, 2007
Museum of Applied Arts, Frankfurt/Main
The teahouse in the museum's garden

190

Zuzana Licko
Marcato (Green/Orange), 2007
From the Puzzler Prints series
Digital Image C-Print, 107 x 72.4 cm, including white border
Published by Emigre
Printed with the Durst Lambda digital laser imager

192

Zuzana Licko

Crescendo (Red/Blue), 2007

From the Puzzler Prints series
Digital Image C-Print, 73.7 x 80 cm, including white border
Published by Emigre
Printed with the Durst Lambda digital laser imager

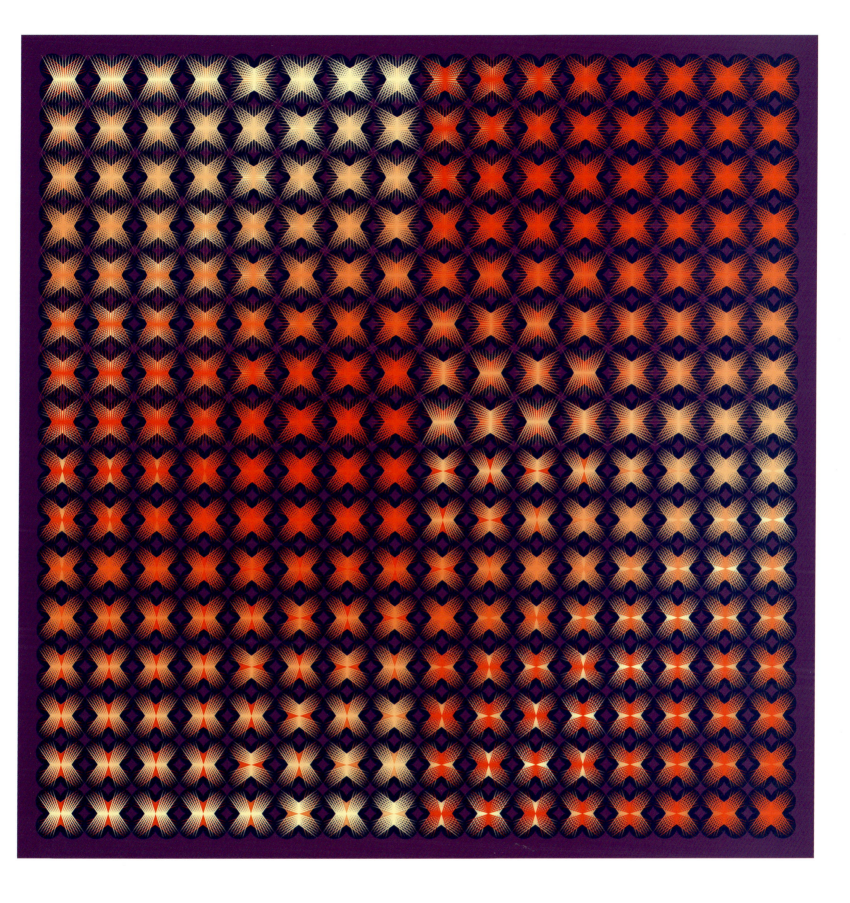

193

Zuzana Licko
Pizzicato (Red/Purple), 2007

From the Puzzler Prints series
Digital Image C-Print, 73.7 x 80 cm, including white border
Published by Emigre
Printed with the Durst Lambda digital laser imager

Harmen Liemburg
Crispy Cloud Kombini Crystals, 2007
Silkscreen on cardboard
Siebold House, Leiden

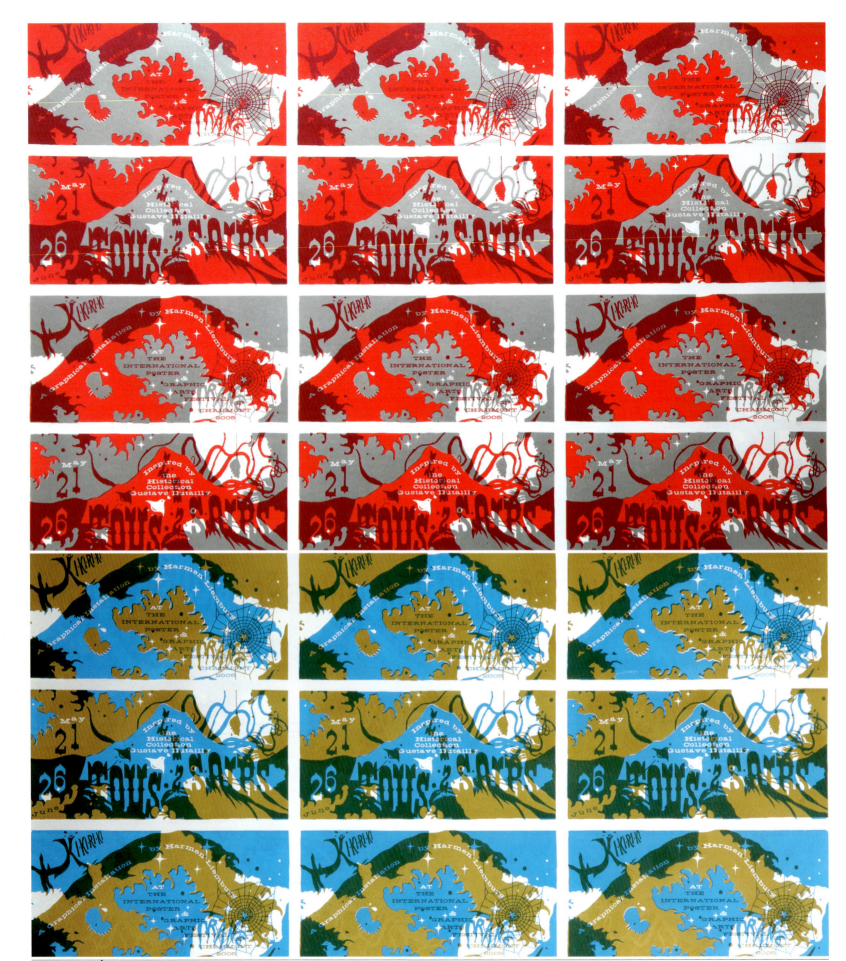

196 **Harmen Liemburg**
Ki Ki Ri Ki, 2005
Invitation card
Silkscreen on cardboard (3/3 colours), 12 x 25 cm, 1200 copies
Festival International de l'Affiche et du Graphisme de Chaumont
above: Printing plate back
below: Printing plate front

Harmen Liemburg
Ki Ki Ri Ki, 2005
Screenprinted poster, 84 x 120 cm
Festival International de l'Affiche et du Graphisme de Chaumont

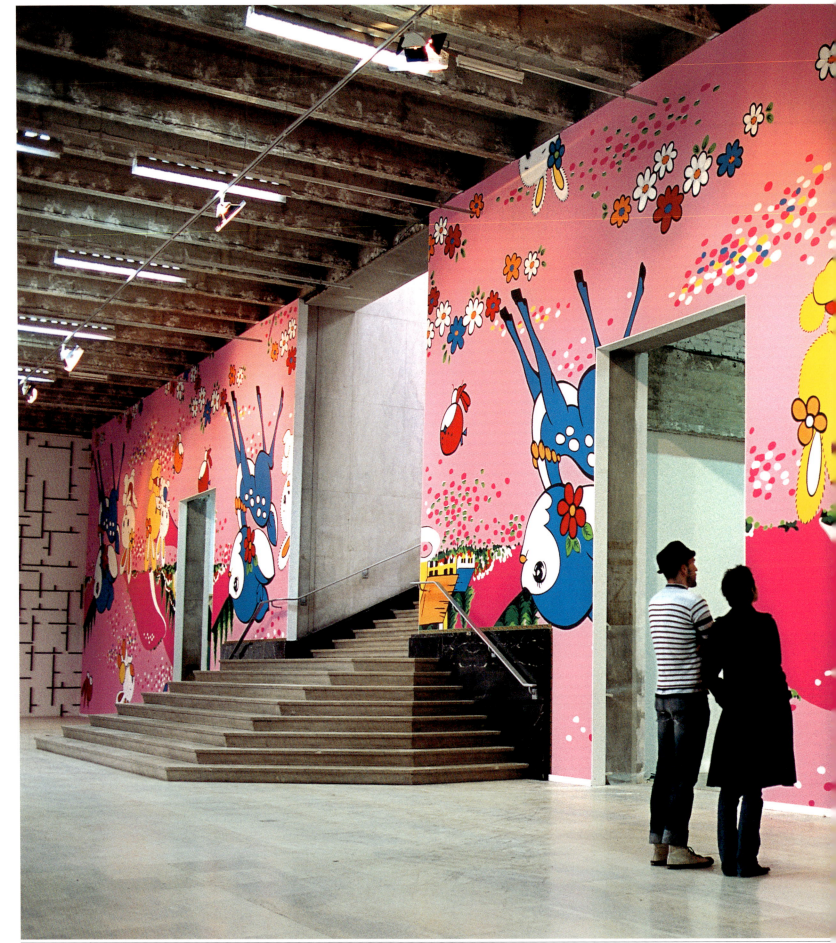

Michael Lin
Untitled, 2006
Acrylic on canvas
Installation view Palais de Tokyo, Site de Creation Contemporaine, Paris
Courtesy of the artist

Michael Lin
The Contemporary Museum, Honolulu, May–December 2005

Emulsion
Tennis court, outdoor installation
The Contemporary Museum, Honolulu, Hawaii
Courtesy of the artist

201 | **Michael Lin**
Quai Rambaud 14.09.–31.12.05, Lyon Biennial 2005
Acrylic on wood

Lydia in St Petersburg
Metal-fabric wallpaper, 2006
Jacquard silk, bronze, patina, manual silkscreen printing

203

Lydia in St Petersburg
Metal-fabric wallpaper, 2006
Jacquard silk, copper, patina, manual silkscreen printing

Ane Lykke
Mind the Gap, 2006
Wall installation made of plastic honeycomb elements, tape, paint
The Danish Design Centre

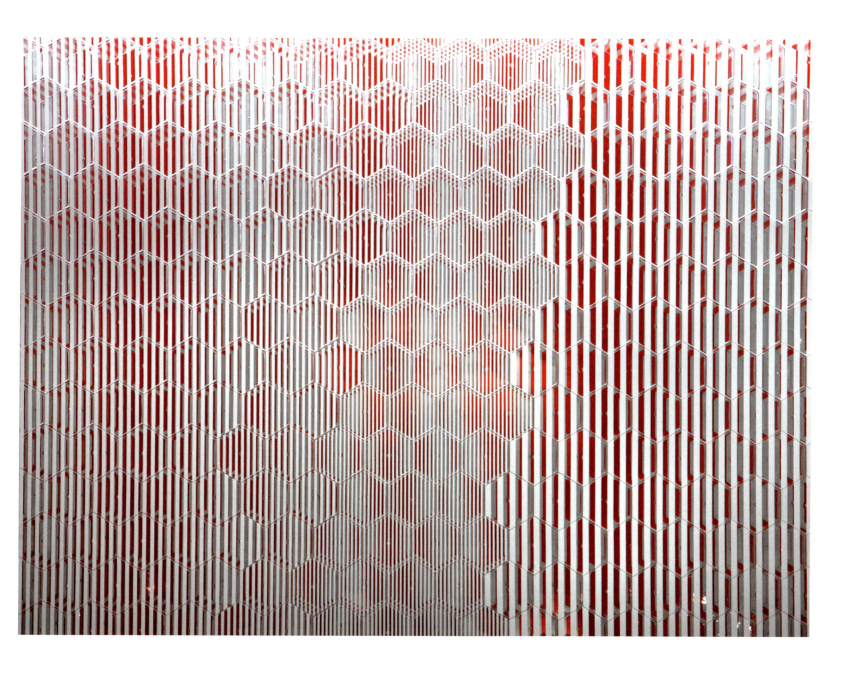

Luna Maurer
The Argyle Pullover, 2004
Machine-knit wool
Luna Maurer, Roel Wouters
Edition of 10 in five different patterns

Barry McGee

Advanced Mature Work, 2007

Installation views Redcat, Los Angeles
Courtesy of Redcat, Los Angeles

Michael Meredith
Ivy, 2007
Coathook system built from Y-shaped plastic units
Manufacturer: Crowley Jones

212 **Michael Meredith**

Huyghe + Le Corbusier Puppet Theater, 2005

Carpenter Center for the Visual Arts, Harvard University, Cambridge, Massachusetts
White polycarbonate, EPS rigid foam, moss
Hardware: CNC router, Software: Rhino
Interior view of the auditorium

214

Michael Meredith

Huyghe + Le Corbusier Puppet Theater, 2005

Carpenter Center for the Visual Arts, Harvard University, Cambridge, Massachusetts
White polycarbonate, EPS rigid foam, moss
Hardware: CNC router, Software: Rhino
Interior view of the stage

215 **Michael Meredith**

Huyghe + Le Corbusier Puppet Theater, 2005

Carpenter Center for the Visual Arts, Harvard University, Cambridge, Massachusetts
White polycarbonate, EPS rigid foam, moss
Hardware: CNC router, Software: Rhino
above: Exterior view
below: The moss covered polycarbonate panels

216 **Igor Mischiyev**
Die Zugereisten (Blue Breuer), 2007

Watercolour on damask (mattress drill), 220 x 125 cm
Courtesy of the artist, Gering & Lopez Gallery, New York,
Galeria Javier Lopez, Madrid

217 | **Igor Mischiyev**
Die Zugereisten (Ghost Dance), 2005
Watercolour on damask (mattress drill), 220 x 110 cm
Courtesy of the artist, Gering & Lopez Gallery, New York,
Galeria Javier Lopez, Madrid

218　**Igor Mischiyev**
Die Zugereisten (Midnight), 2007
Watercolour on damask (mattress drill), 220 x 300 cm
Courtesy of the artist, Gering & Lopez Gallery, New York,
Galeria Javier Lopez, Madrid

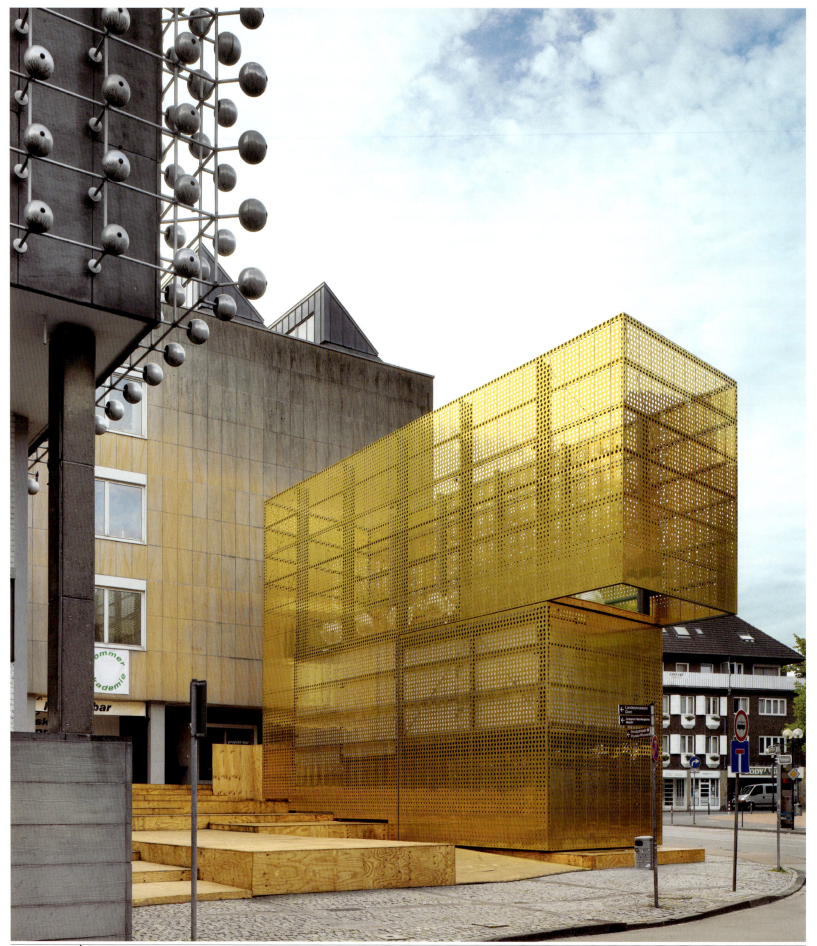

220 | **Modulorbeat**
Switch+, 2007
Information pavilion, Sculpture Projects Münster
Perforated metal with copper-aluminium alloy
Exterior view

Modulorbeat
Switch+, 2007
Information pavilion, Sculpture Projects Münster
Perforated metal with copper-aluminium alloy
Detail of the perforated façade casing

Modulorbeat
Switch+, 2007
Information pavilion, Sculpture Projects Münster
Perforated metal with copper-aluminium alloy
Exterior view by night

Modulorbeat

Switch+, 2007

Information pavilion, Sculpture Projects Münster
Perforated metal with copper-aluminium alloy
Exterior view by night. In the front: Light installation "Silver Frequency"
[Silberne Frequenz] by Otto Piene

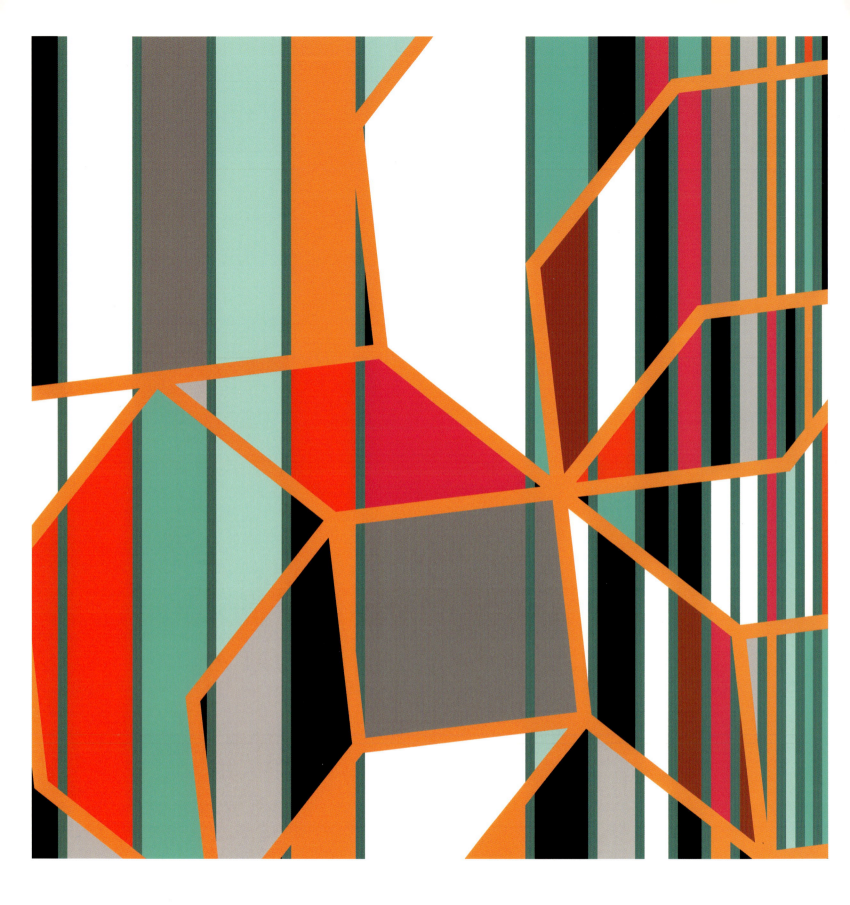

224

Sarah Morris
Viceroy [Los Angeles], 2006
Household gloss on canvas, 214 x 214 cm
Courtesy of Galerie Meyer Kainer

Sarah Morris
Robert Towne [Los Angeles], 2006
Household gloss on canvas, 289 x 289 cm
Courtesy of Galerie Meyer Kainer

Sarah Morris
Artists Management Group [Los Angeles], 2006
Household gloss on canvas, 214 x 214 cm
Courtesy of Galerie Meyer Kainer

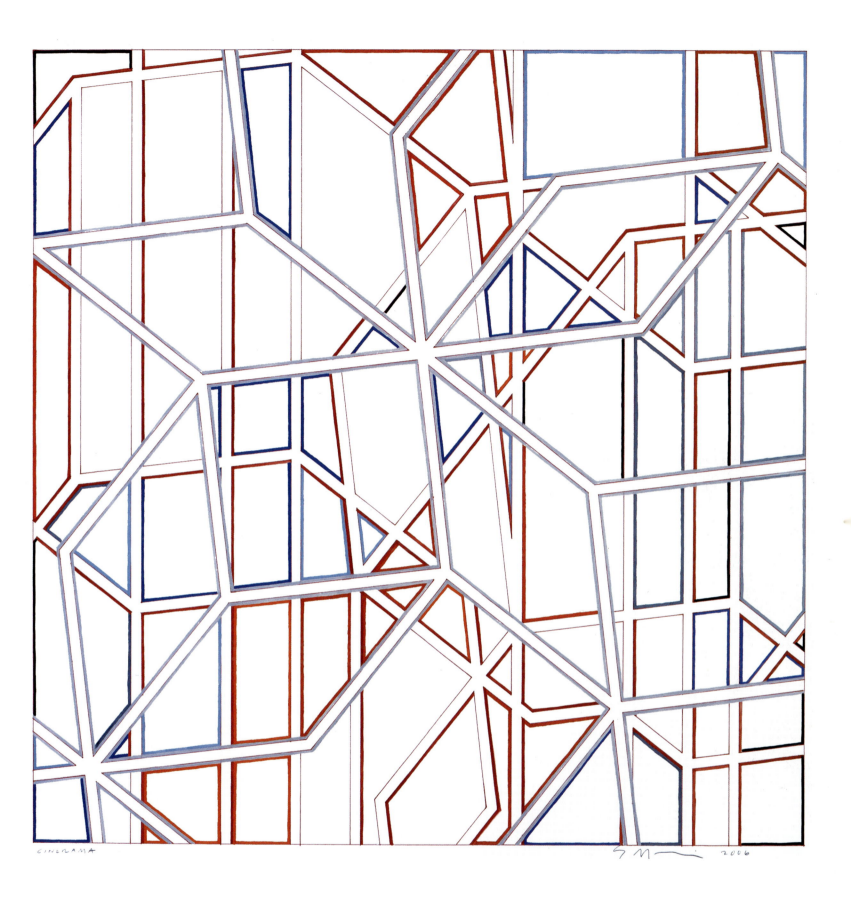

Sarah Morris
Cinerama [Los Angeles], 2006
Ink and gouache on paper, 53.7 x 53.7 cm
Courtesy of Galerie Meyer Kainer

Mount Fuji Architects Studio
Masahiro Harada + MAO

Sakura, Tokyo, 2006
Four-storey residential building
Exterior view of the freestanding walls made of perforated steel

Mount Fuji Architects Studio
Masahiro Harada + MAO

Sakura, Tokyo, 2006
Four-storey residential building
Exterior view of the entrance

230　**Mount Fuji Architects Studio**
Masahiro Harada + MAO

Sakura, Tokyo, 2006
Four-storey residential building
View of the patio lying behind the perforated wall

231 **Mount Fuji Architects Studio**
Masahiro Harada + MAO
Sakura, Tokyo, 2006
Four-storey residential building
Exterior view by night

Marc Newson
Jacket, 2nd G-Star collection, 2005
Front view
Manufacturer: G-Star

233 **Marc Newson**
Jacket, 2nd G-Star collection, 2005
Back view
Manufacturer: G-Star

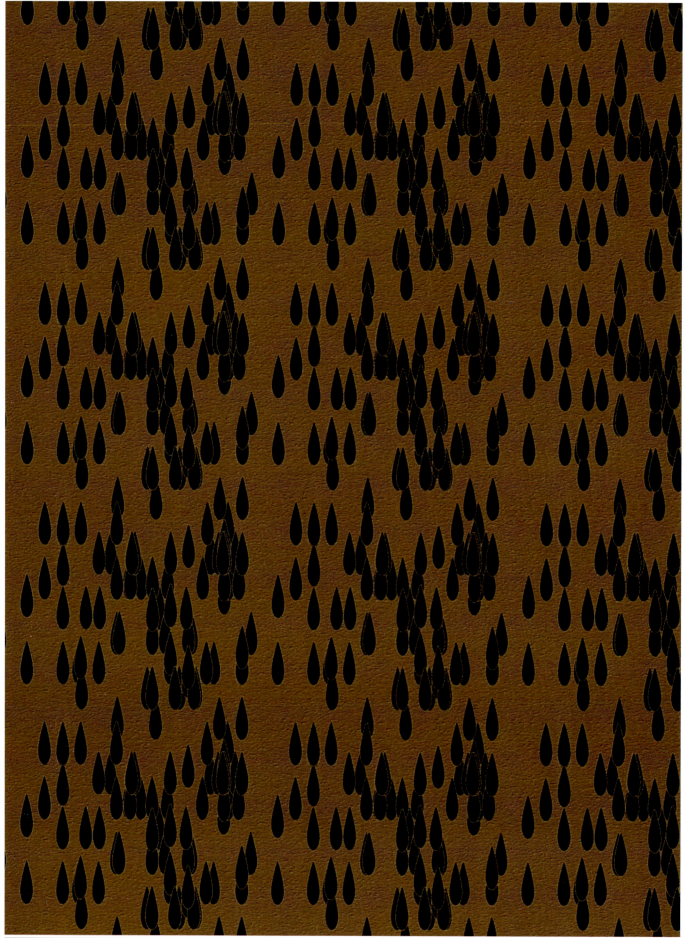

234   **Christopher Pearson**
Bullet
Animated wallpaper, 1050 x 1400 pixels
Design: Timorous Beasties, 2001
Animation: Christopher Pearson, 2006
A Tribe Art Project

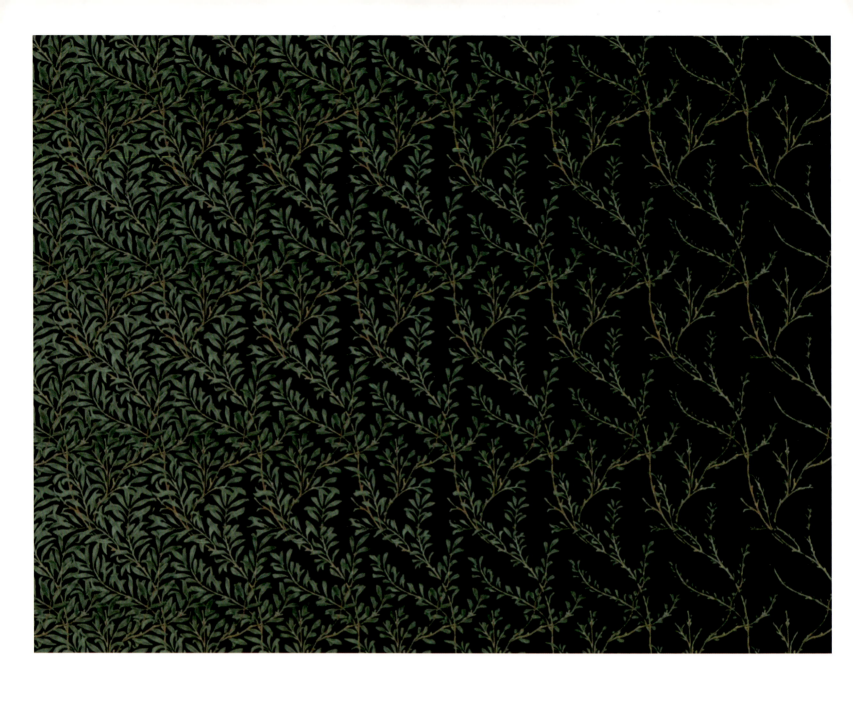

Christopher Pearson
Willow Boughs, 2005

From the "Look At Your Walls" series
Animated wallpaper, 768 x 1024 pixels
Design: William Morris, 1887
Animation: Christopher Pearson, 2005

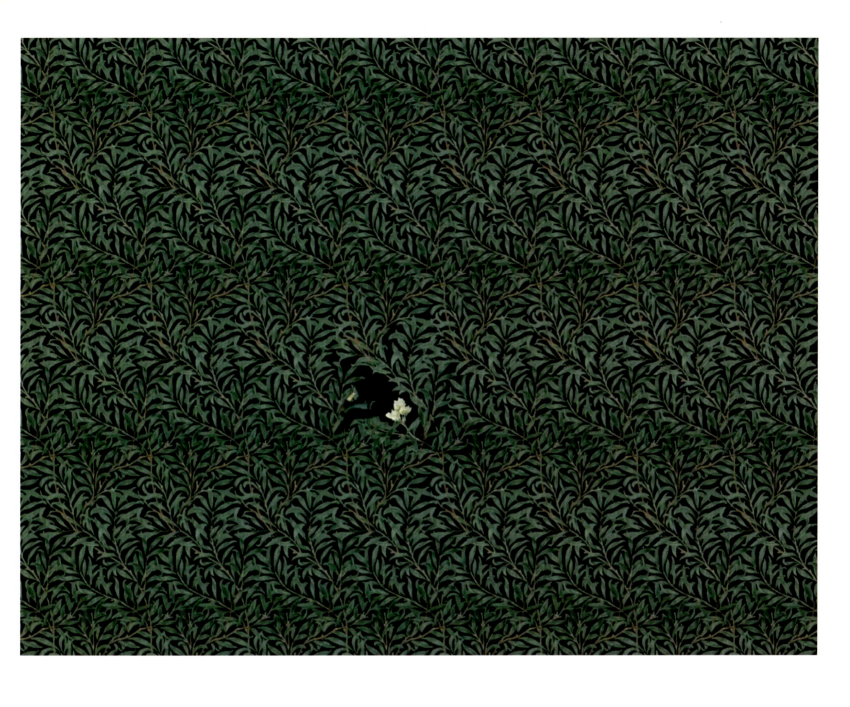

237 **Christopher Pearson**

Willow Boughs, 2006

From the "Look At Your Walls" series
Animated wallpaper, 1024 x 576 pixels
Design: William Morris, 1887
Animation: Christopher Pearson, 2005

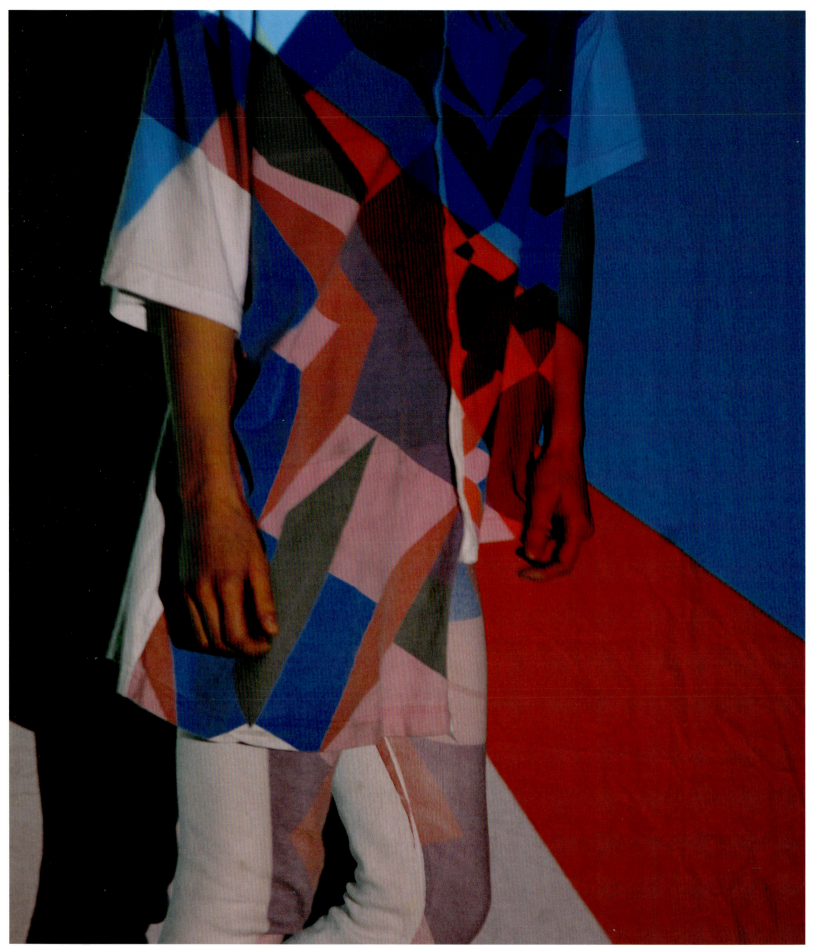

Pipa
Wearables, 2006/07
Graphic prints on paper and fabric

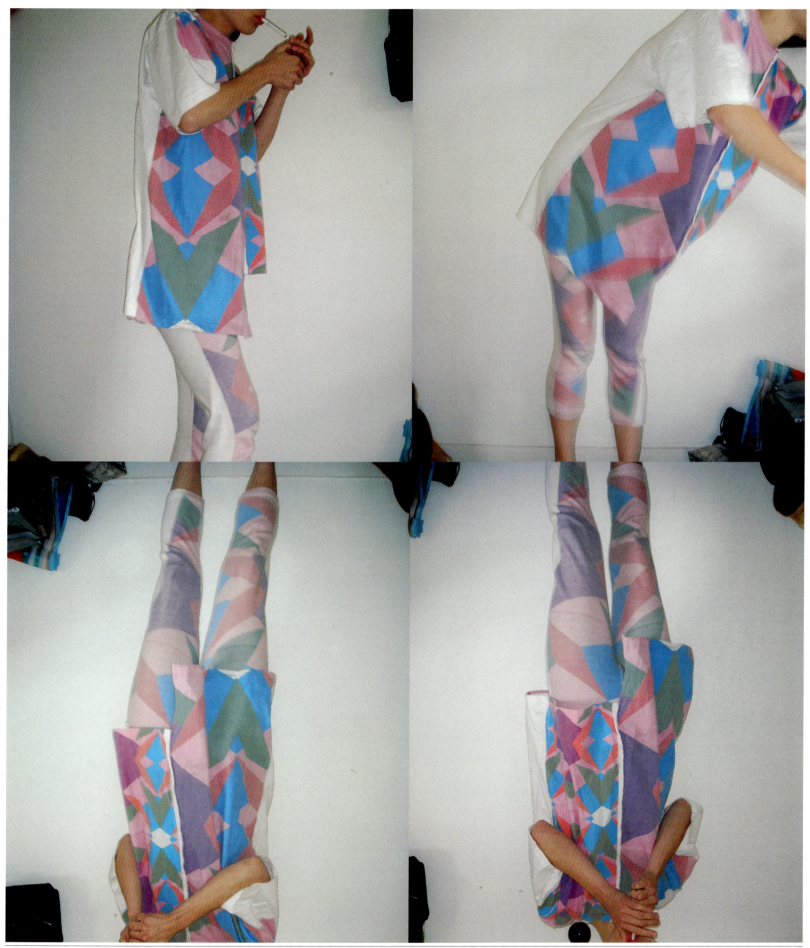

Tobias Rehberger
Installation view "Utterances of a quiet, sensitive, religious,
serious, progressive, young man, who presumes from his deep
inner conviction that he is serving a good cause", 2006

Pigmented polyurethane fast cast resin; joints: acrylic fluorescent dayglow paste
Courtesy of Galerie Bärbel Grässlin, Frankfurt am Main

241   **Tobias Rehberger**
Installation view "Utterances of a quiet, sensitive, religious,
serious, progressive, young man, who presumes from his deep
inner conviction that he is serving a good cause", 2006
Pigmented polystyrene
Courtesy of Galerie Bärbel Grässlin, Frankfurt am Main

Tobias Rehberger
Installation view "Utterances of a quiet, sensitive, religious,
serious, progressive, young man, who presumes from his deep
inner conviction that he is serving a good cause", 2006
Pigmented polyurethane fast cast resin, spray paint
Courtesy of Galerie Bärbel Grässlin, Frankfurt am Main

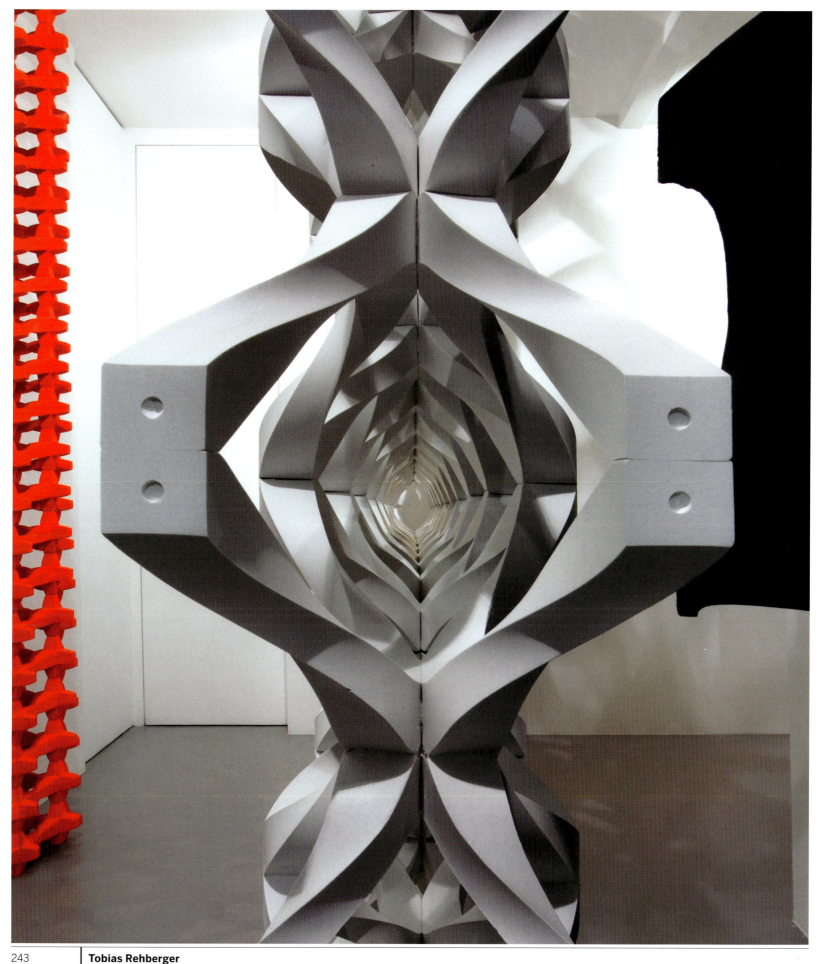

243

Tobias Rehberger
Installation view "Utterances of a quiet, sensitive, religious,
serious, progressive, young man, who presumes from his deep
inner conviction that he is serving a good cause", 2006
Pigmented polyurethane fast cast resin
Courtesy of Galerie Bärbel Grässlin, Frankfurt am Main

Bernd Ribbeck
Untitled, 2007

Ink and ballpoint pen on paper, 35.4 x 25.4 cm
Private collection Germany
Courtesy of Galerie Ben Kaufmann, Galerie Kamm

Bernd Ribbeck
Untitled, 2007

Ink and ballpoint pen on paper, 25.4 x 35.4 cm
Private collection Germany
Courtesy of Galerie Ben Kaufmann, Galerie Kamm

Bernd Ribbeck
Untitled, 2007
Ballpoint pen and acrylic on MDF, 66 x 40 cm
Courtesy of Galerie Ben Kaufmann, Galerie Kamm

247 **Bernd Ribbeck**

Untitled, 2006

Marker pen, ballpoint pen and acrylic on MDF, 50 x 30 cm
Private collection
Courtesy of Galerie Ben Kaufmann/ Galerie Kamm

Clare Rojas
Untitled (3 men & Geodesic dome), 2004
Gouache and latex on wood, 35.6 cm x 27.3 cm

Clare Rojas
Untitled (Girl with Crystals and Bull), 2004
Gouache and latex on wood, 21.6 x 25.4 cm

Clare Rojas
Untitled (Women with Daggers), 2006
Gouache and latex on paper, approx. 23 x 30 cm

251 | **Clare Rojas**
Untitled (Girl in forest with knife), 2004
Gouache and latex on wood, 30.5 x 23.5 cm

Savant
Serum VS Venom (SVSV) Knitwear Collection 2007
Cashmere

Savant
Serum VS Venom (SVSV) Knitwear Collection 2007
Cashmere

256

Annette Schröter
Blick ins Land 2, 2003
Paper cut, 250 x 190 cm
Courtesy of galerieKleindienst, Leipzig

257 **Annette Schröter**
Frau in Waffen I, 2003
Paper cut, 250 x 185 cm
Courtesy of galerieKleindienst, Leipzig

Annette Schröter
Kleiner Rundschnitt 5/07, 2007
Paper cut, cardboard, lacquer, approx. 60 cm
Courtesy of galerieKleindienst, Leipzig

Annette Schröter
Kleiner Rundschnitt 4/07, 2007
Paper cut, cardboard, lacquer, approx. 60 cm
Courtesy of galerieKleindienst, Leipzig

Yinka Shonibare, MBE
Un Ballo in Maschera (Conspirators), 2004

Five life-size mannequins, glass base, Dutch wax printed cotton textile,
leather shoes, 196 x 56 x 43 cm each
Front view
Courtesy of the artist and Stephen Friedman Gallery, London

Yinka Shonibare, MBE

Un Ballo in Maschera (Conspirators), 2004

Five life-size mannequins, glass base, Dutch wax printed cotton textile,
leather shoes, 196 x 56 x 43 cm each
Back view
Courtesy of the artist and Stephen Friedman Gallery, London

Yinka Shonibare, MBE

Un Ballo in Maschera (Courtiers II), 2004

Three life-size mannequins, glass base, Dutch wax printed cotton textile,
leather shoes, 196 x 56 x 43 cm each
Front view
Courtesy of the artist and Stephen Friedman Gallery, London

263

Yinka Shonibare, MBE

Un Ballo in Maschera (Courtiers II), 2004

Three life-size mannequins, glass base, Dutch wax printed cotton textile,
leather shoes, 196 x 56 x 43 cm each
Back view
Courtesy of the artist and Stephen Friedman Gallery, London

Katrin Sonnleitner
Persian Puzzle Rug, 2007
Natural and synthetic rubber, water cut, 1225 pieces per sqm
(size of one piece: 28 x 28 mm)

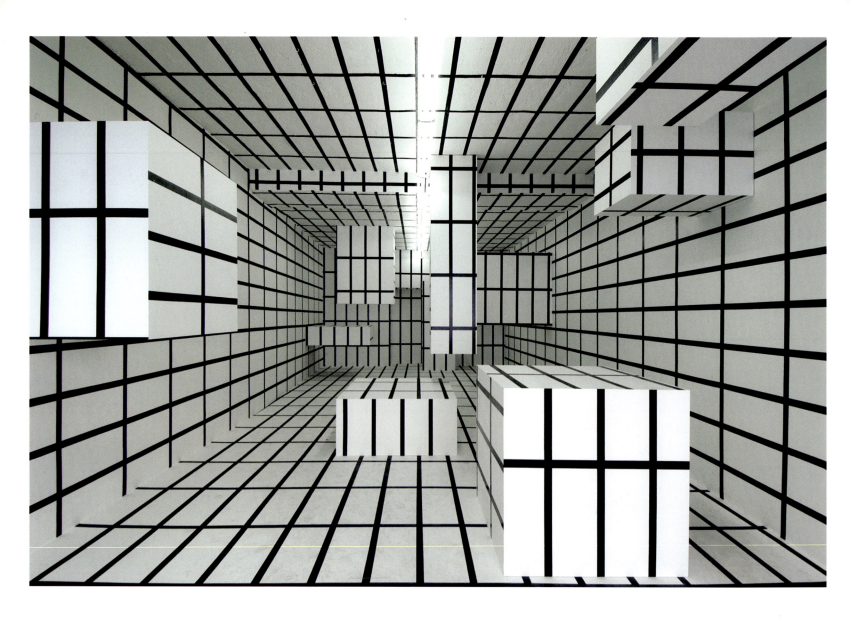

Esther Stocker
Das Wort "gleichartig" zieht unsere Aufmerksamkeit auf sich,
und doch besagt es eigentlich gar nichts. (Frege), 2004

Installation, modules with black masking tape, 13.3 x 5.6 x 3.4 m
Installation view AR/GE Kunst Galerie Museum, Bozen

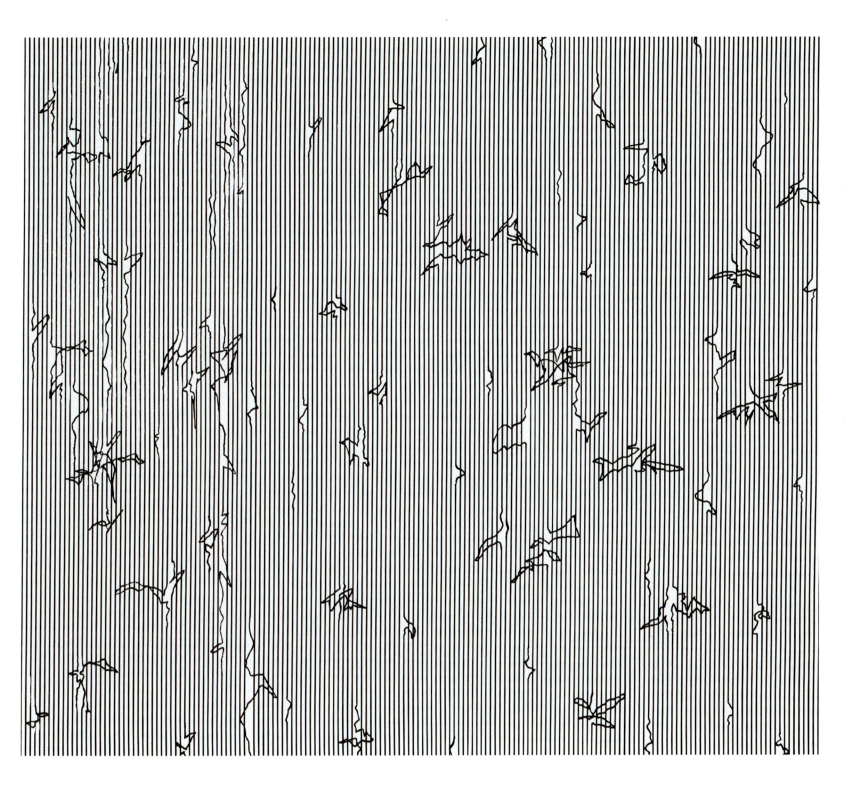

Esther Stocker

Untitled, 2004

Acrylic on cotton, 140 x 160 cm
Courtesy of Galerie Krobath Wimmer

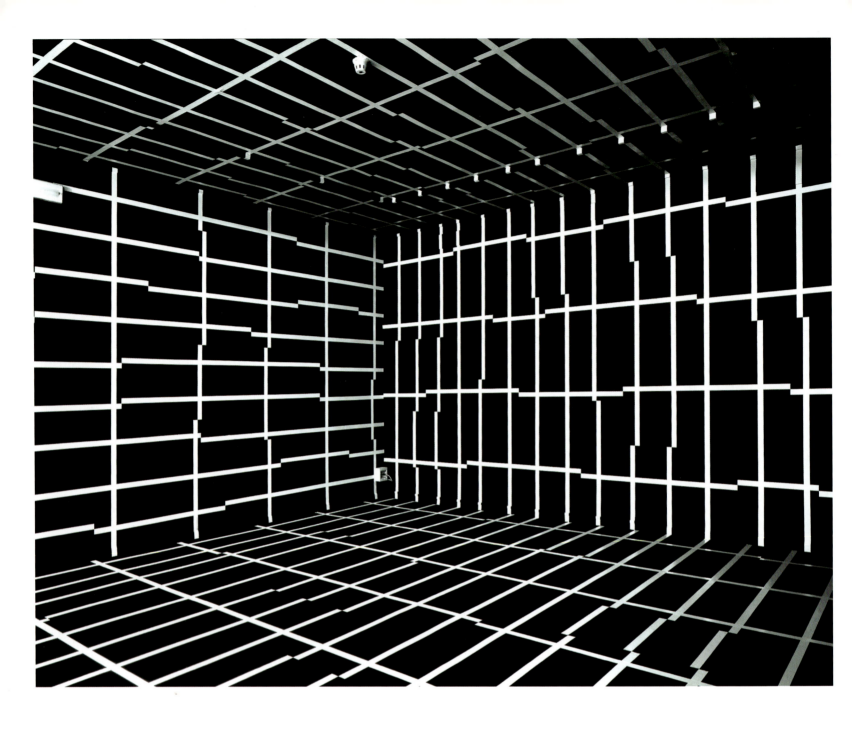

Esther Stocker

Dal punto di vista formale, la parete esiste solo come superficie,
come delimitazione di corpo e spazio; per quanto, in linea di
principio, una faccia della parete non sappia nulla dell'altra.
(Feldtkeller), 2006

Installation, black emulsion and white masking tape on wall and floor,
approx. 7.05 x 6.2 x 4.15 m
Installation view Galleria Contemporaneo, Mestre

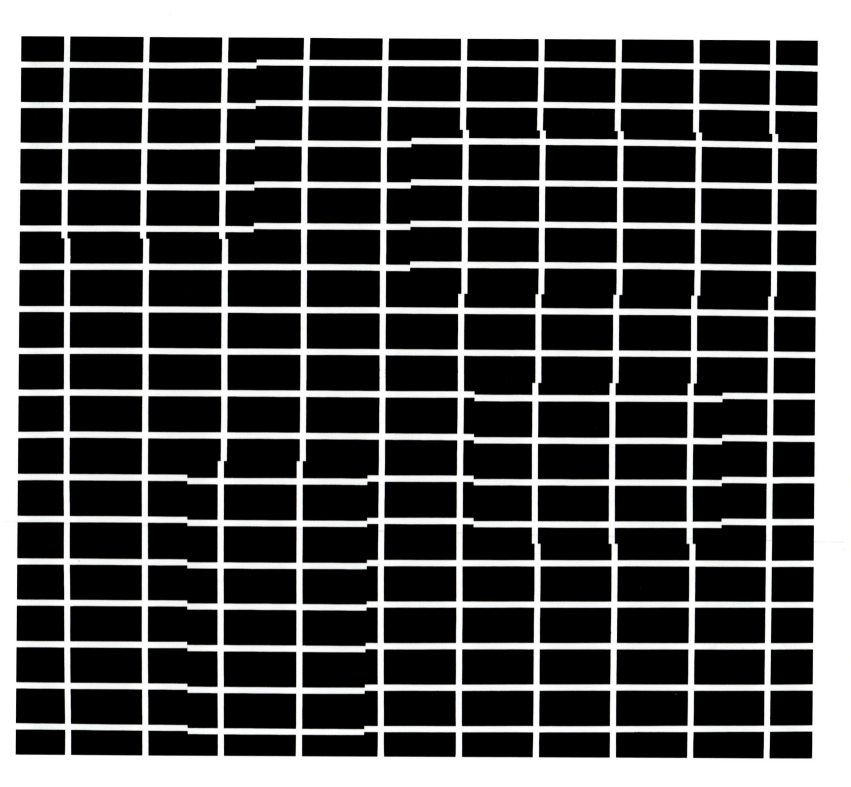

Esther Stocker
Untitled, 2003
Acrylic on cotton, 140 x 160 cm
Courtesy of Galerie Krobath Wimmer

270 **Christine Streuli**

Go North, Go South, Go East, Go West, 2007

Acrylic and gloss paint on cotton, 286 x 371 cm
Courtesy of Galerie Mark Müller, Zurich/Galerie Monica De Cardenas, Mailand, Zuoz/
Galerie Andrée Sfeir-Semler, Hamburg, Beirut

271 **Christine Streuli**
Z Off, 2007
Acrylic and gloss paint on cotton, 268 x 371 cm
Courtesy of Galerie Mark Müller, Zurich/Galerie Monica De Cardenas, Mailand, Zuoz/
Galerie Andrée Sfeir-Semler, Hamburg, Beirut

272 **Christine Streuli**
Strick, 2007
Acrylic and gloss paint on cotton, 140 x 120 cm
Private collection Switzerland

273

Christine Streuli

Krone, 2007

Acrylic and gloss paint on cotton, 120 x 140 cm
Courtesy of Galerie Andrée Sfeir-Semler Hamburg, Beirut

274 **Studio Job**
Insects Pattern, 2004
Fabrics for the Viktor & Rolf Winter Collection 2004/05

Studio Job
Insects Pattern, 2004
Tiles for Royal Tichelaar Makkum

276 **Studio Job**
Gilded narrative screen for the restaurant Matbaren at the
Grand Hôtel Stockholm, 2007
Screen design: Studio Job
Interior design: Ilse Crawford

277

Studio Job
Gilded narrative screen for the restaurant Matbaren at the
Grand Hôtel Stockholm, 2007
Detail

278 **Richard Sweeney**
Icosahedron II, 2006
220 gsm paper, adhesive

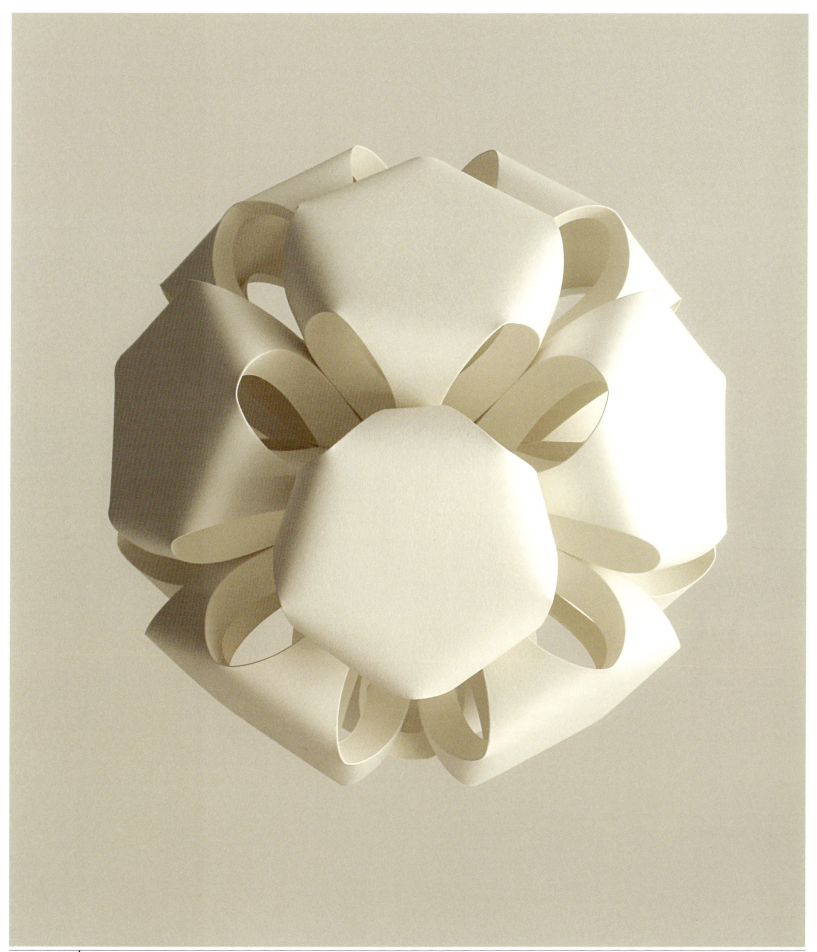

Richard Sweeney
Dodecahedron II, 2006
220 gsm paper, adhesive

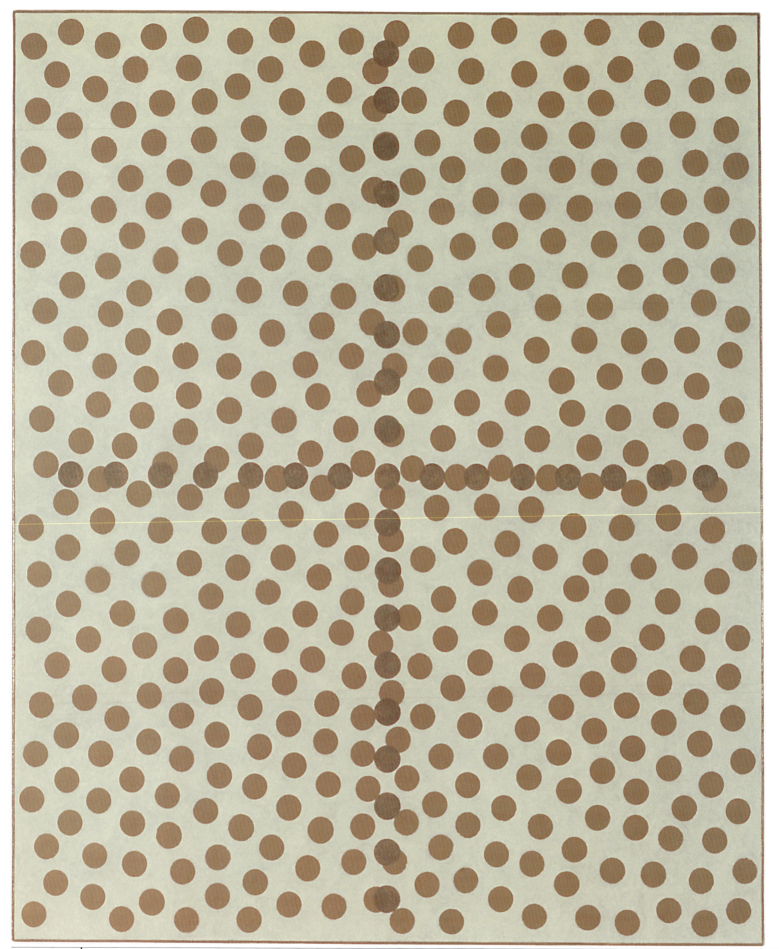

Jon Thompson
Valletta (the final tear), 2005
Acrylic on canvas, 120 x 100 cm
Copyright of the artist
Courtesy of Anthony Reynolds Gallery

Jon Thompson
Valletta (the first cut), 2005

Acrylic on canvas, 120 x 100 cm
Copyright of the artist
Courtesy of Anthony Reynolds Gallery

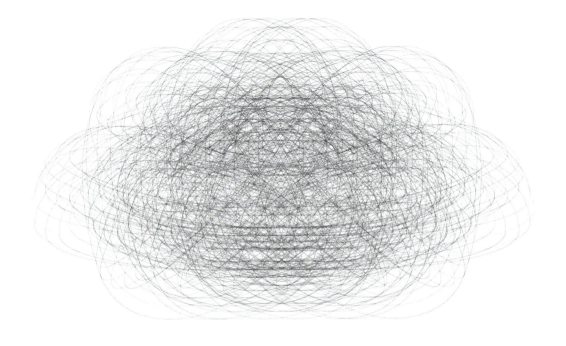

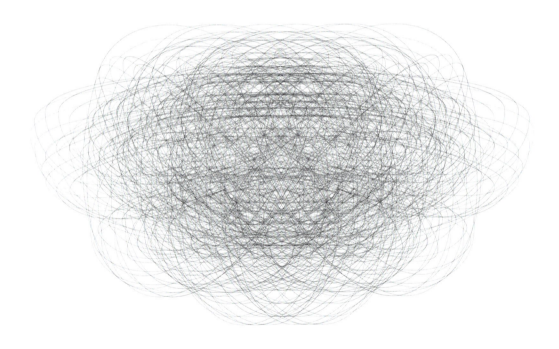

Karsten Trappe
Schwingung 14/08/07, 2007
C-Print, 80 x 80 cm

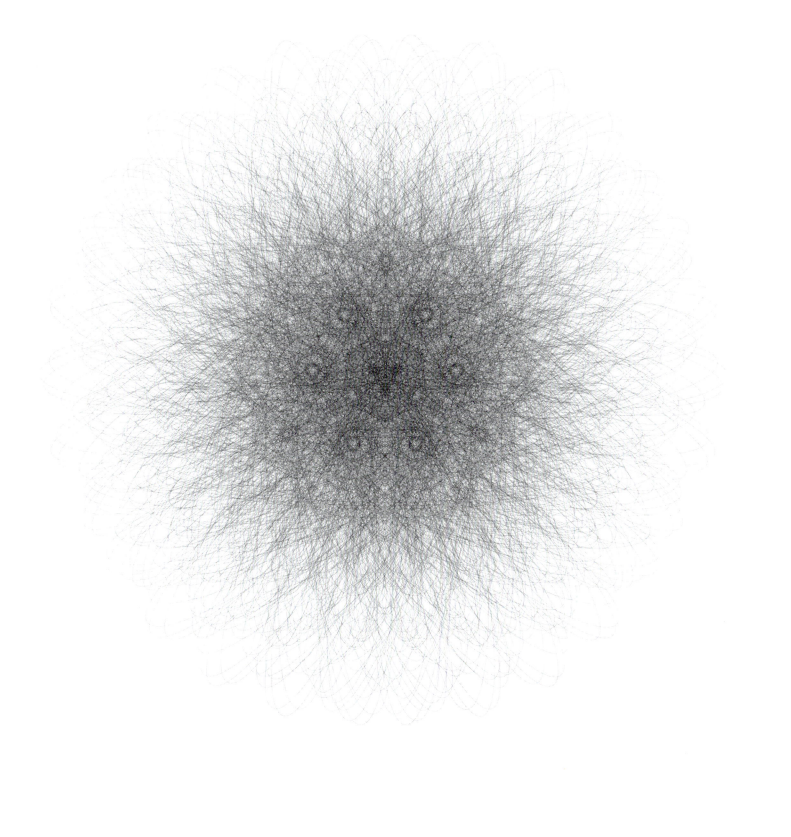

283 | **Karsten Trappe**
Schwingung 04/07/06, 2006
C-Print, 80 x 80 cm

Karsten Trappe
Schwingung 02/07/06, 2006
C-Print, 80 x 80 cm

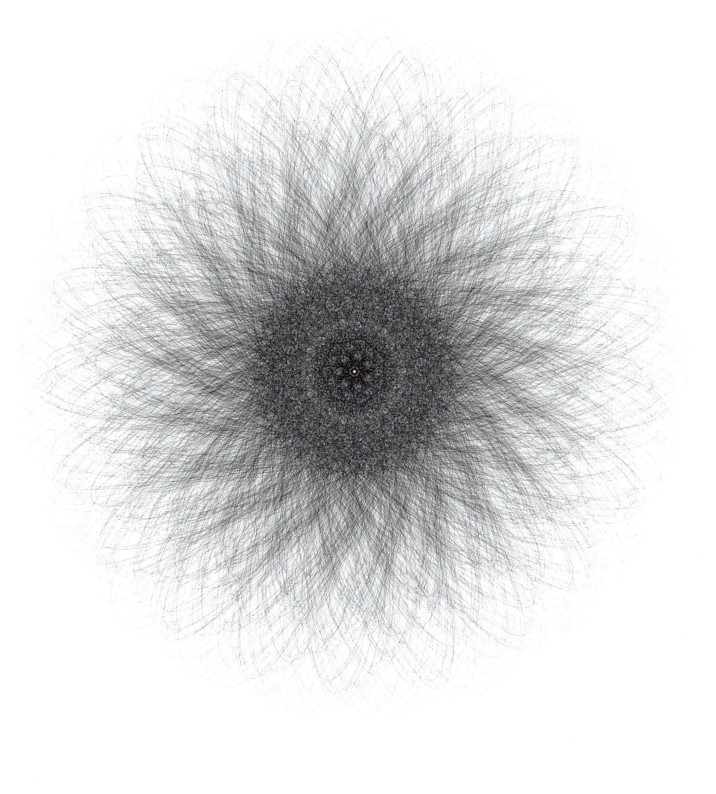

285 | **Karsten Trappe**
Schwingung 01/07/06, 2006
C-Print, 80 x 80 cm

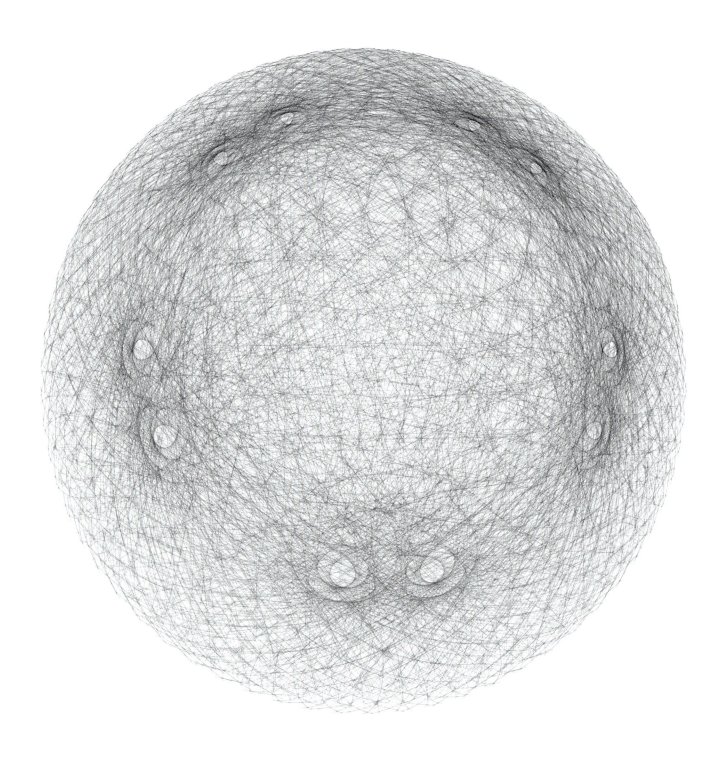

Karsten Trappe
Schwingung 28/08/07, 2007
C-Print, 80 x 80 cm

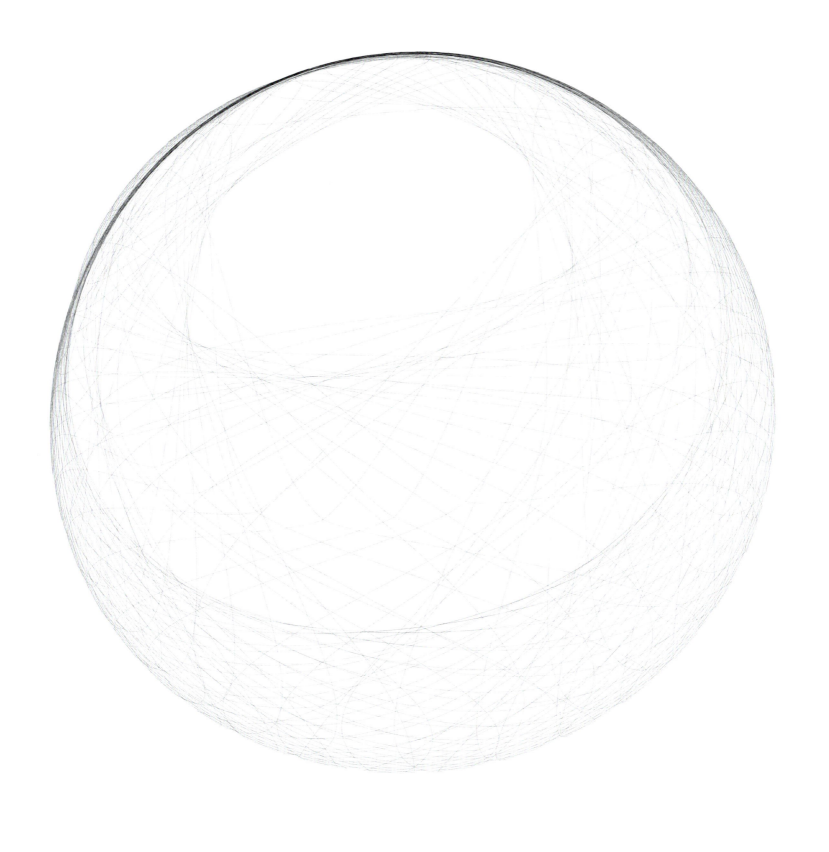

287 **Karsten Trappe**
Schwingung 14/08/07, 2007
C-Print, 80 x 80 cm

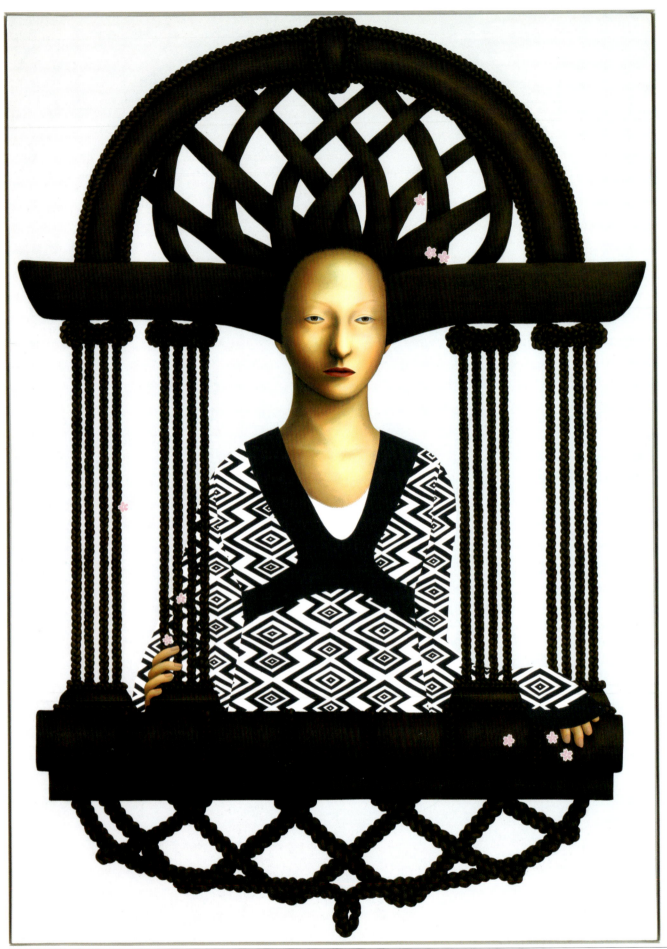

Aya Uekawa
Japanese Anti-Asian, 2007
Acrylic on panel in artist frame, 142.5 x 107.5 cm, framed
Private Collection USA

Aya Uekawa

The Japanology Web (Second World Complex Series), 2007

Acrylic on panel, 127 x 91.4 cm
Collection of Susan Hancock
Courtesy of Kravets/Wehby Gallery, New York

Aya Uekawa
The Noncommittal Girl, 2006
Acrylic on panel, 112 x 112 cm
Ovitz Family Collection, Los Angeles
Courtesy of Kravets/Wehby Gallery, New York

Aya Uekawa
A Euro Lover, 2006
Acrylic on panel, 102 x 76 cm
Private Collection, New York
Courtesy of Kravets/Wehby Gallery, New York

Patricia Urquiola
ideal house cologne, 2005

imm cologne, Koelnmesse
Installation view

Patricia Urquiola
Antibodi, 2006
Manufacturer: Moroso

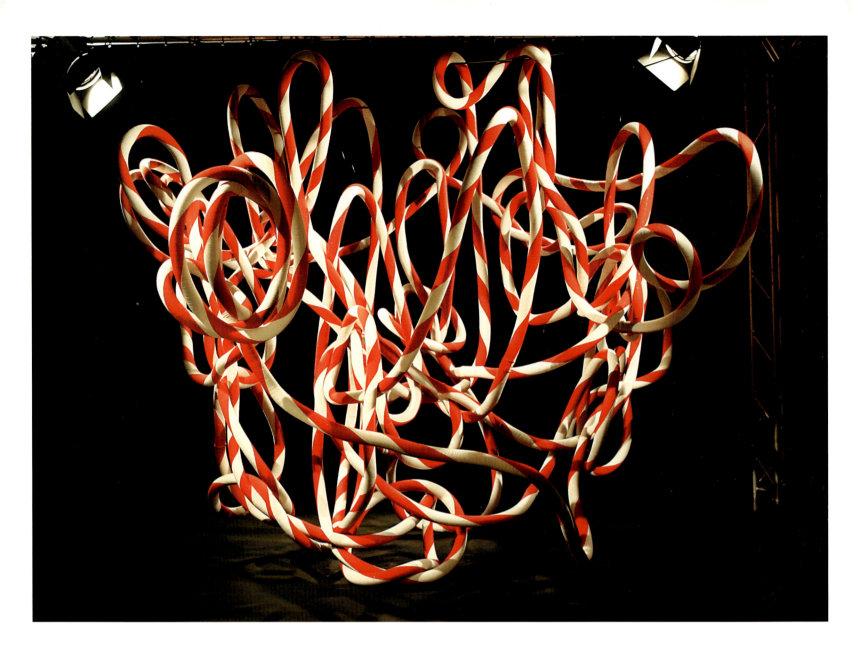

Henrik Vibskov
Cyklys
Men's autumn/winter collection 2006/07

Henrik Vibskov
Fantabulous Bicycle Music Factory
Men's spring/summer collection 2008

300   **Henrik Vibskov**
The Black Carrots Collection
Men's autumn/winter collection 2007/08

Miguel Vieira Baptista
Figo, 2003
Hand tufted carpet, 300 x 190 x 1.5 cm
Limited edition of 50 pieces
Loja da Atalaia Gallery, Lisbon

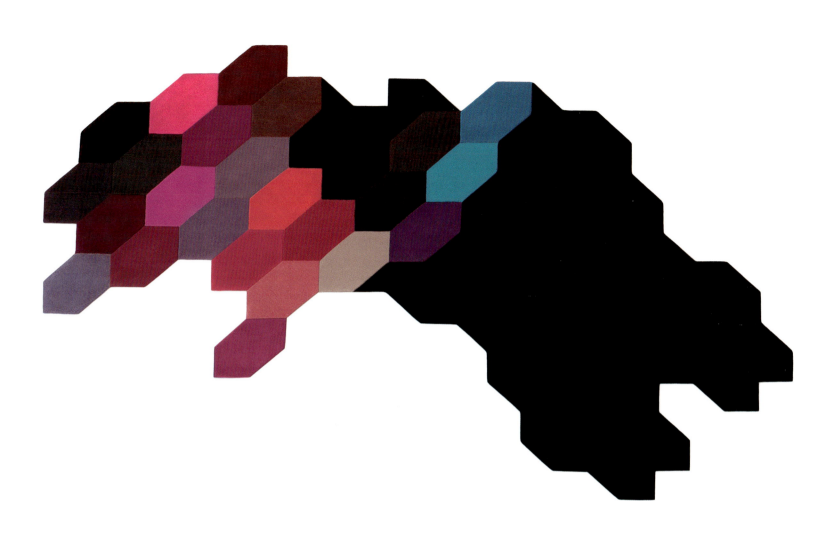

Miguel Vieira Baptista
Mancha, 2007
Hand tufted carpet, 290 x 175 x 1.5 cm
Limited edition of 50 pieces
Cristina Guerra Gallery, Lisbon

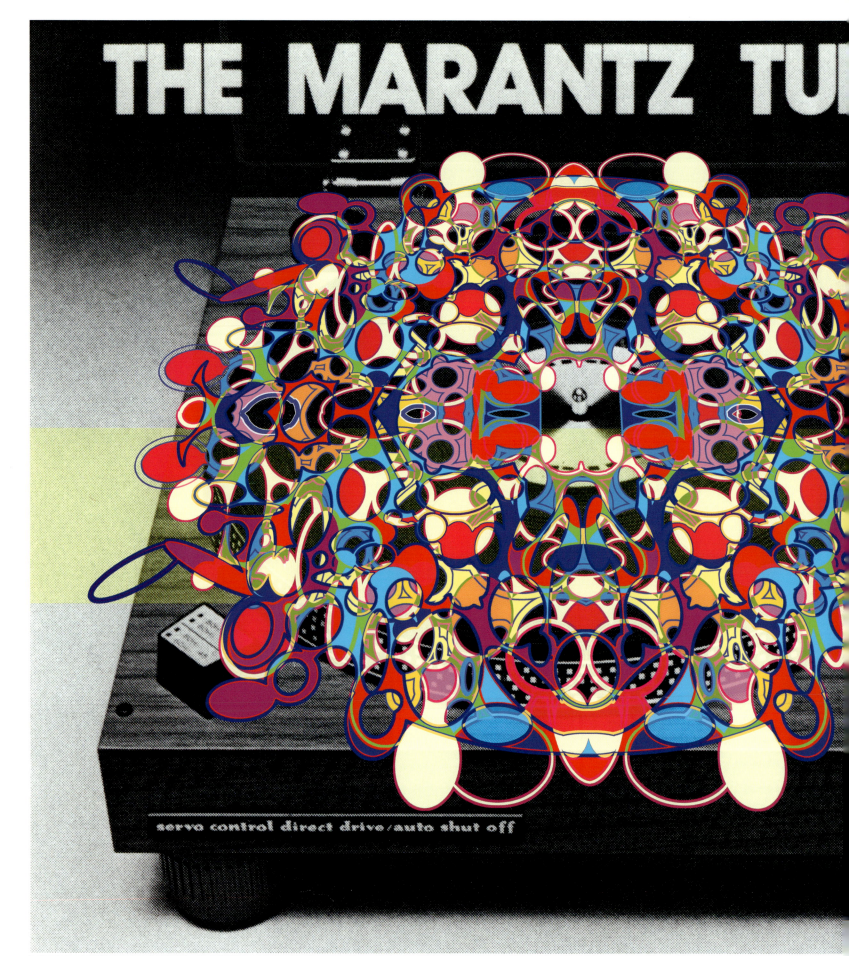

Kelley Walker
Marantz Model 6300 with Yellow Stripe, 2004
CD-Rom with digital print, dimensions variable
Courtesy of the artist and Paula Cooper Gallery, New York

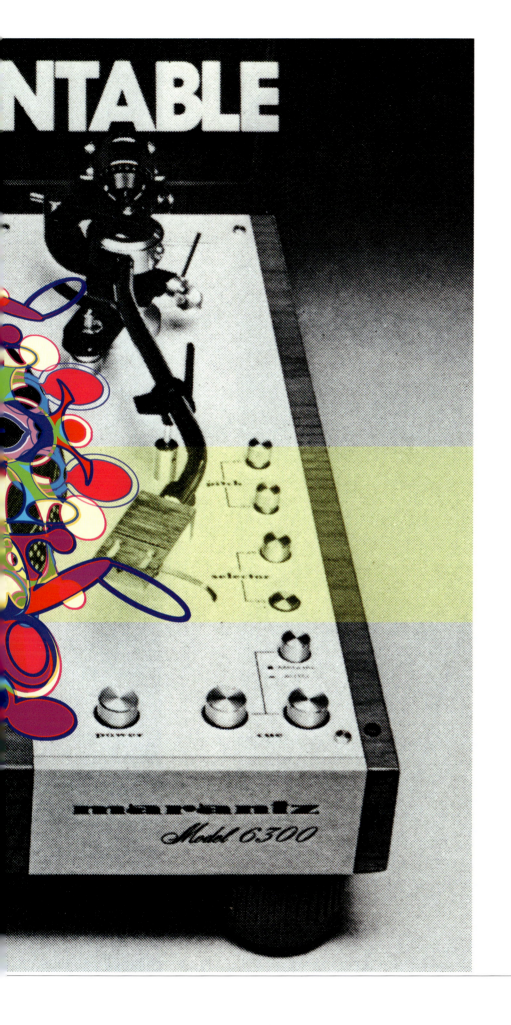

306

Kelley Walker

Maui, 1988, 2002

CD-Rom with digital print, dimensions variable
Courtesy of the artist and Paula Cooper Gallery, New York

Marius Watz
System C, Drawing 1, 2005
Created by generative software system

310

Marius Watz
Packing 02, 2007
Created by generative software system

312 | **Bernhard Willhelm**
Spring/Summer Collection 2008

Bernhard Willhelm
Spring/Summer Collection 2008

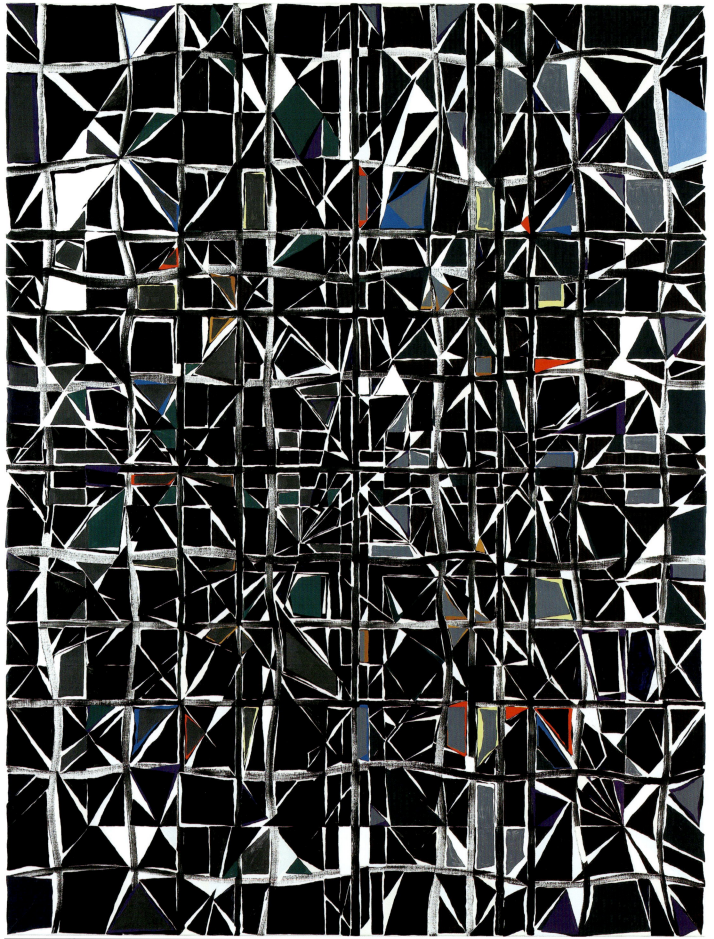

Mette Winckelmann
Crystal Mirror, 2006
Acrylic on canvas, 180 x 140 cm
Courtesy of Galleri Christina Wilson

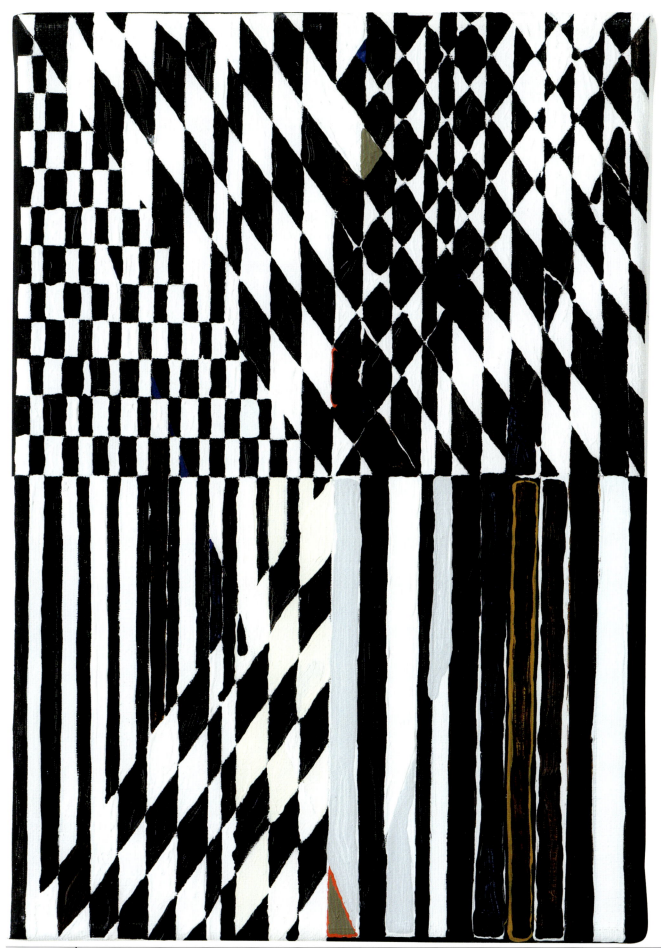

317 **Mette Winckelmann**
Untitled, 2006
Acrylic on canvas, 30 x 21 cm
Courtesy of Galleri Christina Wilson

318 **Mette Winckelmann**
Ethnic Behaviour, 2006
Acrylic on canvas, 150 x 120 cm
Courtesy of Galleri Christina Wilson

Mette Winckelmann
Untitled, 2006
Acrylic on canvas, 30 x 21 cm
Courtesy of Galleri Christina Wilson

Michael Young
Dr. James Cosmetic Surgery, Taipei, Taiwan, 2005
Interior design and chairs: Michael Young
Wall in Corian with graphic pattern: Katrin Olina

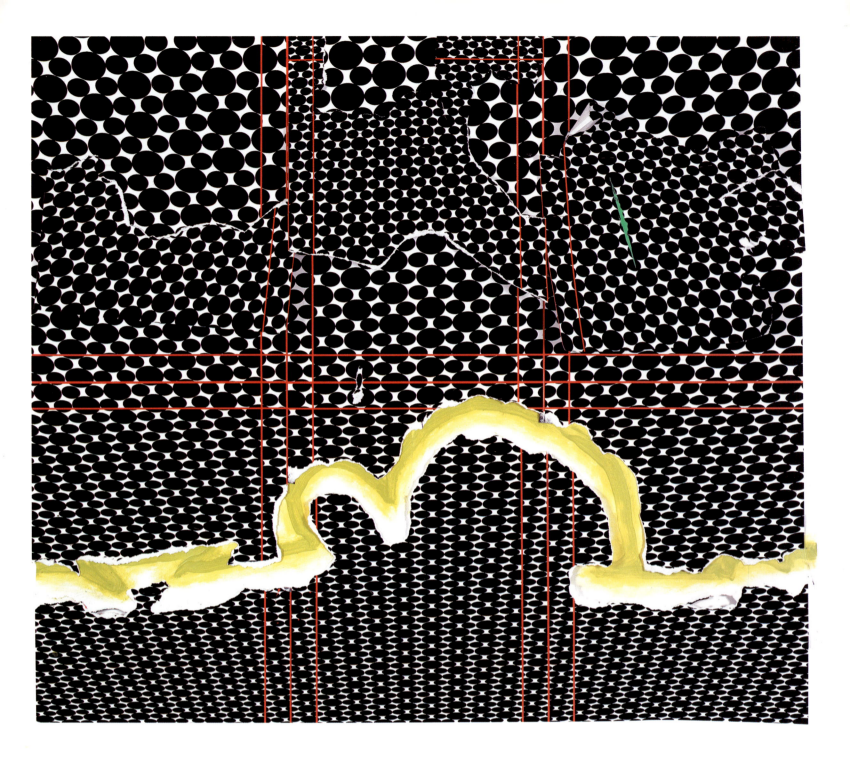

Toby Ziegler
The Subtle Power of Spiritual Abuse (Study), 2007

Inkjet on paper, oil paint, gesso, pins, 128 x 155 cm
Courtesy of Simon Lee Gallery, London

Toby Ziegler

The Subtle Power of Spiritual Abuse, 2007

Oil paint, ink and gold leaf on canvas, 210 x 242 cm
Courtesy of Simon Lee Gallery, London

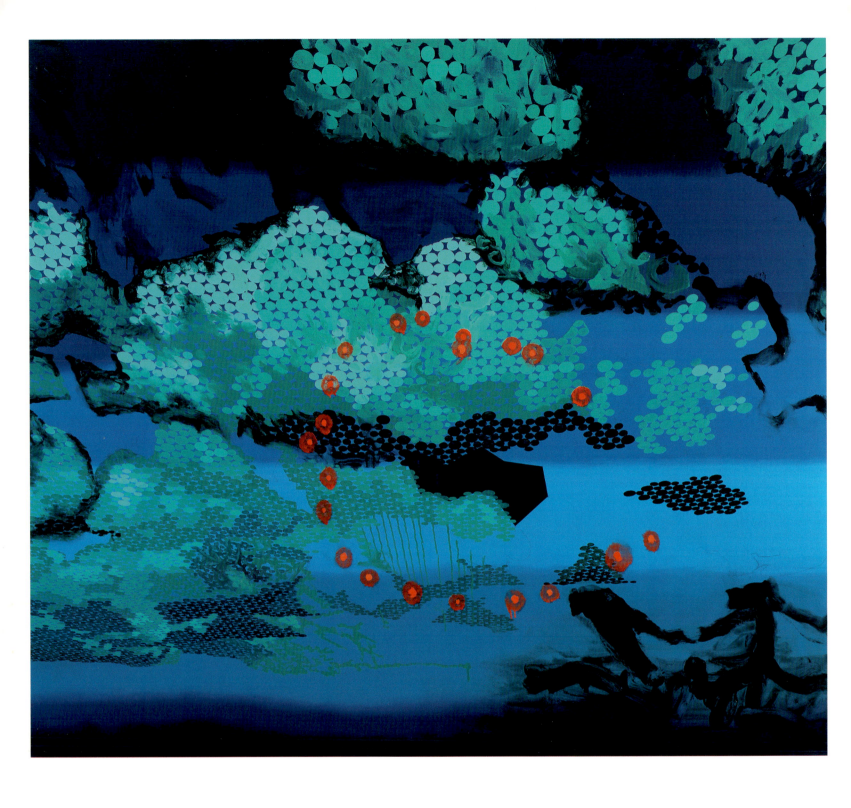

324

Toby Ziegler

Vitalis, 2007

Oil and pencil on canvas, 210 x 242.5 cm
Courtesy of Simon Lee Gallery, London

Toby Ziegler

Sad Cowboy, 2007

Oil on canvas, 210 x 242 cm
Courtesy of Simon Lee Gallery, London

A

Hitoshi Abe

The architect Hitoshi Abe, born in 1962, has had an office in Sendai since 1992. He is the director of the architecture and design laboratory at Tohuku University.
www.a-slash.jp
www.tokolo.com

14/15 Japanese pachinko parlours are real game centres, full of gaudy and kitschy neon advertising. Hitoshi Abe's design for Tiger is something quite different. The only decoration in this pachinko parlour is its façade. Analogous to the ball-bearing in the pachinko machines, the architect sets the façade also visibly "in motion" with adeptly designed optical tricks like flicker effects, geometrical patterns and their subtle variations. Abe conceived this pattern together with the Japanese artist and graphic designer Asao Tokolo. The façade consists of square slabs a metre long on each side, which are attached to the building by being placed in front of a steel frame construction. The elements are made of perforated metal sheets, in which circular segments are traced, so that circular patterns become visible at a distance. It is part of the intended confusion that the circles dissolve in some areas into meandering lines, which irritate the way the viewer perceives them.

Anni Albers

Anni Albers (1899–1994), born in Berlin, directed the weaving workshop at the Bauhaus before emigrating together with Josef Albers to the USA in 1933 to teach at the progressive Black Mountain College near Asheville, North Carolina.

16–19 Woven items and hangings are the hallmark of Anni Albers' oeuvre. As early as in 1949 the Museum of Modern Art in New York honoured her work with an exhibition. At that time she attained the recognition of weaving as a fine art form. Later on Anni Albers turned away from the textile design, which had built her reputation. The two abstract prints "Red and Yellow Meander" are part of her late oeuvre. Her lithographies and screenprints show influences from her travels to Mexico and to Latin America.

Nikos Alexiou

The Greek artist Nikos Alexiou was born on Crete in 1960 and is currently based in Athens.
www.nikosalexiou.com

Nikos Alexiou is obsessed with historic patterns. In his work, he time and again starts out from Byzantine mosaic floors, using their rapports for projections and superimposing them as an immaterial pictorial layer over large-format computer prints or gigantic paper cut-outs. In his installations, the artist often makes use of natural materials such as paper, bamboo, straw or wood chips. The fragility of these materials amplifies the expression and effect of his filigree patterns.

20–23 For his installation "The End", which he exhibited in the Greek pavilion at the 2007 Biennale in Venice, he repeatedly visited the Monastery of Iviron on Mount Athos. He projected the patterns found there over paper silhouettes and records of his artistic work and research.

24/25 On the occasion of an exhibition in the European Patent Office in Munich, Nikos Alexiou, inspired by the mosaics at the Iviron Monastary, produced an extremely delicate paper silhouette.

Jun Aoki

The Japanese Jun Aoki studied architecture in Tokyo and was subsequently employed in the offices of Arata Isozaki, where he collaborated with Shigeru Ban, among others. He opened his own studio in 1991, also in Tokyo. In 2005, the Japanese Office for Art and Culture honoured him for his works.
www.aokijun.com

26–29 Jun Aoki's small wedding chapel is situated at the centre of a lake. Its structure of intertwined steel rings between a glass front on the outer side and translucent material on the inside alludes to the wedding couple's exchanging of rings. The formation of rings also provides stability sufficient for breaking up the closed form. The play of lights which develops at night between the illuminated façade, the surface of the water and the inside room is striking. The White Chapel is part of the Hyatt Regency Hotel in Osaka.

Kevin Appel

The American artist Kevin Appel is based in Los Angeles, California.

30–33 As a painter, Kevin Appel is preoccupied with the difficult relationship between nature and modernist design or architecture. Combining sections from check or stripe patterns with elements reminiscent of wood veneer, he creates dizzying picture puzzles. The wooden elements scattered across his paintings make his "clouds of patterns" look like bushes and trees. In his way of painting, too, he is guided by design and architecture. He transfers the perfectionist and smooth surfaces familiar to us from building façades or from industrial products to his own work. Thus we seek the painterly brush stroke in vain – the smoothness of his style much rather resembles forms of machine production.

B

Neil Banas

Neil Banas is an oceanographer based in Seattle.
www.neilbanas.com

34–37 Neil Banas develops visualisations for biological processes such as the formation of swarms in plankton. He programs interactive applications that allow for the adaptation of parameters and the calculation of effects. And vice versa, he uses his work as a source of inspiration for his free graphical works – patterns, for instance, in which the colour, running down invisible hills, seems to obey the laws of nature. Banas' patterns are also available in the form of printed wallpaper.

Barber Osgerby

Edward Barber and Jay Osgerby studied architecture at the Royal College of Art in London and have been collaborating since 1996.
www.barberosgerby.com
www.therugcompany.info

38–41 Edward Barber and Jay Osgerby designed an ornament made of intertwining circles and applied it to very different materials and functions: for The Rug Company, the designers used it in small scale for a woollen rug, designing different colour ranges with six colours each. In the shops of fashion designer Stella McCartney, the ornament features in the three-dimensional structure of the "Starflower" ceramic tiles.

Barkow Leibinger Architekten

The architects Regine Leibinger and Frank Barkow established their Berlin studio in 1993.
www.barkowleibinger.com

42/43 The company Trumpf specialises in laser-based metalworking. For the company's head office in Ditzingen, the Barkow Leibinger studio designed a showpiece featuring this technology: an unsupported roof equipped with a backlit, welded honeycomb structure projects 20 metres from the gatehouse beyond the drive, illustrating the company's capabilities.

44/45 Regine Leibinger and Frank Barkow designed the Trutec company office building for the Digital Media City in Seoul – one of the numerous city neighbourhoods devised on a drawing-board during the Asian building boom. The eleven-storey building quite literally reflects this specific situation in its fragmented mirror façade, which continually shows a kaleidoscopic image of its surroundings. During the day, the view into the interior of the building changes as does the reflection of the environment on the mirror surfaces. The façade is constructed of only two basic modules, each 2.70 metres wide, divided into different polygonal segments, rotated and tilted.

David Best

David Best (born 1954) is an artist based in San Francisco, California.

46/47 The American artist David Best constructs theatrical temples and chapels from banal everyday objects or remains from industrial production. Their richly ornamented surfaces are a particularly striking aspect of his fairy tale buildings. For this committed advocate of public art, the work process is paramount. The construction of his buildings therefore always doubles as a happening and as an exercise in self-awareness.
David Best's name is also closely connected to the Burning Man arts festival in the Nevada desert. Every year, tens of thousands of people make their pilgrimage to the Black Rock Desert, a remote desert two hours north of Reno, in order to be part of a festival of performances, interactive installations and fire art. The spectacle culminates in the setting ablaze of a large manlike statue – the "Burning Man". For this event, Best designed some of his most pompous buildings, such as the Temple of Honor (2003). At the end of the festival, his pieces too are put to the flames.

Max Bill

Max Bill (1908–1994), born in Winterthur, was an architect, artist and designer. He founded the famous Ulm School of Design and was its first Rector.

48–51 After completing his studies at the Bauhaus Dessau, Max Bill went to Zurich. His artwork there made him one of the best-known representatives of the "Zurich Concrete Artists", who were for their part influenced by Constructivism and the Dutch group "De Stijl". The horrors of the Second World War had an unmistakable influence on Bill's work. That is the reason for the emphasis in his work on formulating an idealised, socio-political worldview. His allies on this path were Inge Scholl and Otl Aicher, with whom he founded the legendary School of Design in Ulm in 1951. Bill was active in all areas. Regardless of whether he was building houses, designing products, producing sculptures or painting, he always went about his work like a technician. He analysed a problem and then found a solution. And so his declaration describing works of art as "objects for intellectual use" is also no more than fitting. Alongside the famous Ulm stool, a piece still being produced in unaltered form today and capable of serving as a tray and a side table, his painting, graphics and sculptures are highly significant.
As a typical representative of concrete art, Bill orientated himself according to science and tried to transfer the clarity of mathematics and geometry onto his works.

Matthias Bitzer

The artist Matthias Bitzer was born in Stuttgart in 1975; he is currently based in Berlin.

52–55 Matthias Bitzer's works stand at the junction between abstract and figurative representations, where he often cites the representational style and events of the early 20th century. His works repeatedly refer to historical characters somewhat marginal to history, whose life experience he adapts into a magically and mystically charged cosmos of images. He preserves these persons – such as the co-founder of Dada, Emily Ball-Hennings – from being forgotten by portraying them, while draping a veil of ornamentation over them.

Blocher Blocher Partners

In 1989, Jutta and Dieter Blocher established their studio for architecture, retail design and corporate design in Stuttgart.
www.blocherblocher.com

56–57 The spectacular façade of the department store ac/ces owned by the company Engelhorn in the German city of Mannheim stands out due to its wedge-shaped windows, which open wide towards the street intersection. At the same time, the triangular expanses allow a view from an unusual angle into the interior of the building. Inside, the expressive design continues, with the edges of the ceilings having been separated from the façade. The architects' intention was to comment on the characteristic relationship between desirability of luxury brands on the one hand and their understatement on the other by means of an extravagant sequencing of open and closed spaces.

Tord Boontje

The designer Tord Boontje was born in 1968 in the Dutch city of Enschede and studied design in Eindhoven und London. Since 2005 he has been living in Bourg-Argental, France.
www.tordboontje.com

58–61 Tord Boontje became known for his laser-cut filigree floral patterns rendered from such diverse materials as metal, Tyvek or felt into lamps and room dividers. In his sketches entitled "Watercolor", the symmetry of which reminds one of the ink blobs in Rorschach tests, Boontje again combines high-tech and craft: "I like using the digital printing techniques for the creation of organic shapes. This form of mirroring could not possibly be produced by painterly means, but it is possible with the computer."

Chris Bosse

Chris Bosse, who was born in Stuttgart, now lives as an architect in Sydney, where he also teaches at the University of Technology as an Innovation Fellow. He designed the "Water Cube" swimming stadium in Beijing, which will serve as a competition venue in the 2008 Olympic Games.
www.chrisbosse.de

62/63 For some years, Chris Bosse has been working on organic structures, which he generates on the computer. He studies natural forms such as foams or rhizomes and later translates them into loadbearing structures or façades. For this particular piece of work, "Digital Origami", he asked his students at the University of Technology to design a small module capable of serving as the basic skeletal unit for complex structures – comparable to the micro-organisms of coral reefs. The installation, initially planned on a computer, resulted in 3,500 cardboard models of two different shapes, which were then fitted out with LED lights (Erco) and piled up to form a fantastical cavernous landscape.

Ronan and Erwan Bouroullec

The brothers Ronan (1971) and Erwan Bouroullec (1976), born in the French town of Quimper, have been collaborating as designers from 1999. Their clients include Ligne Roset, Magis and Vitra.
www.bouroullec.com

Through their room dividers, the brothers Ronan and Erwan Bouroullec investigate the possibilities of using textiles as architectural elements. Their room dividers are flexible as well as stable, decorative and sound absorbent. The pattern emerges when individual modules are fitted together.

64/65 The voluminous room dividers designed by the brothers for the German-Swiss company Vitra are named "Roc" – as in rock. In this project they make use of a modular system of sheets of cardboard. However, the cut of the individual elements only allows for a single formation. The system is not flexible in any way.

66/67 The "North Tiles" from the textile manufacturer Kvadrat are slotted into each other and can form level or curved surfaces. Originally set up in the Kvadrat showroom in Stockholm, they were also put to a different purpose: the designers used the modules to display the company's fabric collection.

Alison Brooks Architects

The Canadian Alison Brooks founded her architectural practice in London in 1996.
www.alisonbrooksarchitects.com

68–71 Herringbone is the classical zigzag pattern we know from materials or from parquet floors. The architect Alison Brooks has rediscovered it for the façade of her Herringbone Houses. The structured wooden façade means that the large mass of the buildings appears very much lighter. In addition, the architect adopts the pattern for so many elements like such as fences, terraces and interior rooms, and in this way gives the buildings their overall comprehensive appearance.

Daniel Buren

The French artist Daniel Buren was born in 1938 and lives in Paris.
www.danielburen.com

72–77 Daniel Buren is regarded as one of the most famous of post-war artists. In the 1960s he developed his style of painting, based chiefly on a repetition of vertical stripes, as a form of critical engagement with traditional painting. To him, stripes are not a form of decoration, but rather a "visual tool" serving him in his investigations into the conditions of art: how it is presented in museums and galleries as well as in public spaces. A banner of stripes, which he had designed for the Guggenheim Museum in New York, and which was to be suspended in the famous rotunda across the entire height of the building, caused controversies and, at the time, was taken down after only one day. His second installation specific to this site took place in 2005 and his "The Eye of the Storm: Works in situ by Daniel Buren" was no less monumental than the first. Instead of the painted-on stripes, however, Buren made use of the structure provided by the building's architect Frank Lloyd Wright. By simply by setting up a mirror expanse he achieved the transformation of the rotunda levels into a gigantic image of stripes.

Sun Young Byun

Sun Young Byun is an artist based in Seoul.

78/79 Sun Young Byun's pleasant interiors are reminiscent of the richly ornamented rooms by Henri Matisse. The artist almost completely desists from depicting spatiality and adds layer upon layer of surfaces resembling paper cut-outs. She creates spatial depth exclusively through textures: patterned shapes are complemented by images within images and alternate with elements left blank.

C

c.neeon

Clara Leskovar and Doreen Schulz are fashion designers. In 2002 they founded the fashion label c.neeon in Berlin.
www.cneeon.de

80–83 Geometrical patterns govern the designs by the c.neeon fashion designers. With their autumn/winter 07/08 collection "Sharing Secrets", Leskovar and Schulz refer to the oeuvre of paintings by Polish artist Tamara de Lempicka: they combine fragmented geometrical patterns in green, pink, red and blue with various shades of grey. Folds in the jersey material then newly break up the opulent Neo-Art-Deco prints.

Chalet 5

Since 1996 Zurich artists Karin Wälchli (born 1960) and Guido Reichlin (born 1959) have been collaborating under the name of Chalet 5.
www.chalet5.ch

84–87 For many years Chalet 5 have been working on comprehensive studies of ornaments. Having previously investigated the separation of patterns from their cultural context, they now dedicate much of their work to the interaction of pattern and background. Following a study visit to Cairo where they did extended research into daily life in Egypt, the artists came to adopt a form of sculpture or relief, which combines with the mural painting in the background of the image to form a complex pattern.

Bjorn Copeland

Bjorn Copeland (born 1975) lives and works in New York. The artist studied sculpture at the Rhode Island School of Design.

88–91 In his works, Bjorn Copeland displays an impressive range of narrative collage. Inspired by Surrealism and Op Art, his way of working places patterns at the foreground – as strictly geometrical repetition with a small rapport at times, then again as an amorphous collection of shapes. A closer view reveals layers of newspaper shreds, in between faces looking towards the observer.

Mia Cullin

Mia Cullin studied interior architecture and furniture design at the Konstfack in Stockholm. Since then the designer has done design work for the Swedish furniture company IKEA, among others, as well as for architecture studios.
www.miacullin.com

92/93 Her work "Flake" was created in 2006 for the Finnish design company Woodnotes. The material employed, Tyvek, consists of high-density, non-woven polyethylene fibres as used, for instance, in protective clothing. From this raw material Cullin produces small white flakes that can be linked up at will through the holes she then inserts, thus forming creative patterns for tablecloths or net curtains. The elements can easily be combined to different shapes.

D

Jacob Dahlgren

The artist Jacob Dahlgren was born in Stockholm, Sweden, in 1970.
www.jacobdahlgren.com

94/95 In his works, Jacob Dahlgren time and again comes back to ordinary, everyday objects: scales, yoghurt pots and clothes hangers serve him – neatly arranged in stripes, rectangles and grids – as the basic material for his installations and tableaux. His visual idiom quotes the various trends in 1960s art, be it Op Art, Constructivism, Minimal Art or Pop Art. His installation "I, the world, things, life", shown in 2007 at the Biennale in Venice, is characteristic of his way of working in that it evokes the graphical patterns of Op Art as well as Jaspers Johns's famous Pop Art work "Targets".

Thomas Demand

Thomas Demand was born in 1964 in Munich. The artist lives in Berlin.
www.thomasdemand.de

Thomas Demand's large-format studio photographs display perfectly illuminated rooms, which the artist has replicated in the original scale from coloured paper and cardboard. These rooms are always references: Demand works in keeping with documentary images from press or forensic photography.

96/97 The piece "Studio" shows a room with a table and chairs, a sparse, faceless place where some press conference or other might take place. The significant patterning of the striped wallpaper causes irritation and it indicates the room's origins. We are looking at the recording studio of the game show "Was bin ich?" [What am I?], broadcast by German television from the mid-1950s into the late 1980s.

98/99 A counter-programme to the white cube: for the exhibition of his photographs in the London Serpentine Gallery in 2006, Thomas Demand got a manufacturer to produce wallpaper on old printing blocks and had an ivy pattern in different colours overgrow the interior rooms.

100/101 The photo-wallpaper shows the replica of a decorative façade assembled from cast concrete parts like the ones used in the GDR for buildings made from prefabricated slabs. In the installation Thomas Demand situates it opposite of a concrete wall suspended from the ceiling.

Liz Deschenes

Liz Deschenes was born 1966 in Boston. Today the artist, a photographer by training, lives and works in New York.

102–107 The moiré effect overtaxes eyes and brain; the layering of two regular grid surfaces results in a flickering perception of the image. In the age of offset printing, moiré is an irritating flaw. Liz Deschenes allows this irritation to cover vast surfaces. Her moiré pictures are the size of cinema posters. All are unique and the superimposed patterns are as different as fingerprints. For the exposure, Deschenes uses two negatives each time, positioned at an angle to each other.

Dieter Detzner

Dieter Detzner was born in the German town of Aalen in 1970. Today the artist lives in Berlin.

108–111 Dieter Detzner's constructivist crystal objects are expansive structures. Initially, Detzner begins his work on the computer; he then works on the colours with paper and cardboard models before going on to construct the bodies from materials such as acrylic glass and mirror surfaces. To his interest in the formal repertoire of avant-garde modernist movements he thus adds experiments on material qualities and surface structure. In addition to the calculated effects of reflective surfaces, Detzner also repeatedly works with sources of light, which he integrates into his sculptures. His preferred titles are personal names such as André, Robert or Gabriele. They are supposed to express the individual "character" of a sculpture.

Birgit Dieker

The German artist Birgit Dieker (born 1969) studied sculpture at the University of the Arts in Berlin, where she still lives and works today.

112–115 Pieces of clothing are always vehicles of memory too. They refer to people and to their individual biographies. An aura of anonymous fates therefore surrounds Birgit Dieker's sculptures, which she fashions from numerous layers of cast-off clothing. Time and again, she forms anthropomorphic shapes from the clothes of unknown people. "Olga" is one of them, casually posing with her hands in her pockets like a model, entirely covered with a harlequin-pattern of diamond shapes. The artist breaks up the pleasant, soft bodies by drilling into the layers of material and thereby exposing them. Penetrating the entire body, these "injuries" appear sinister and violent, turning the cheerful production into its opposite. No less sombre are Dieker's death's head, "La Vie en Rose (II)", or her gigantic tornado of cast-off clothing "Wirbel".

E/F

FAT

The architectural studio FAT (Fashion, Architecture, Taste) was established in 1995 in London by Sean Griffiths, Charles Holland and Sam Jacob.
www.fashionarchitecturetaste.com

116/117 An unremarkable building from the 1960s housed the Sint Lucas Art Academy in the Dutch city of Boxtel. FAT were commissioned to undertake alterations to the building. In addition to a new floor plan, they also designed a spectacular façade intended to lend the school its own distinctive identity. Prefabricated parts made of reinforced concrete now hint at the origins of Sint Lucas Art Academy as a monastic school. The architects combine such architectural detail with geometrical patterns by Belgian monk and architect Hans van der Laan, whose coloured surfaces structure interior and exterior walls and are taken up again in the design of the entrance gates.

Thom Faulders Architecture/Studio M

The architect Thom Faulders is based in San Francisco; he designed the façade of the residential and office building Airspace Tokyo in collaboration with the design studio Proces2. The building's architect Hajime Masubuchi has been running his own practice Studio M in Tokyo since 2003.
www.beigedesign.com
www.proces2.com
www.s-t-m.jp

118–121 Thom Faulders designed a bold outer skin for the four-storey building Airspace Tokyo. The screen façade is constructed in two layers from laser-cut aluminium and plastic composite sheets, a material which is also used in noise insulation. The irregular net structure of the façade was generated by parametric software – thereby Faulders makes direct reference to this particular location. Before the construction of the new building in the Tokyo district of Kitamagome Ota-ku, the site was occupied by a residence surrounded by dense greenery, securing the residents' privacy. The screen façade is designed to fulfil the same function.

Foreign Office Architects

The London studio Foreign Office Architects was founded by Farshid Moussavi (born 1965) und Alejandro Zaera-Polo (born 1963) in 1995.
www.f-o-a.net

122–125 Foreign Office Architects created a latticework of 10,000 hexagons to encase the Spanish Pavilion at the 2005 World Expo in the Japanese city of Aichi. The hexagonal elements of the grid were made of glazed ceramics, a technique traditionally employed in the Mediterranean as well as in Japanese architecture. The colour range shows variations of national colours, referring to a popular perception of Spain: bullfighting and red wine, sun and sand. Moreover, the tiled lattices are intended to evoke Gothic rose windows, the architecture of the late Gothic cathedrals in Toledo, Seville and Palma and Islamic architecture. A particular effect was achieved by never repeating the respective arrangement of the various elements, resulting in a pattern that constantly varies slightly.

Herbert W. Franke

Herbert W. Franke, born in 1927, is a philosopher and, among other things, a writer, a speleologist and a co-founder of the Ars Electronica.

126–131 Herbert W. Franke's works are situated at the junction of art, science and technology. One part of his work is dedicated to "cybernetic aesthetics", a form of pictorial representation that uses the computer as a tool and that he has practised since the 1970s. One example for this research is the series "Drakula", an acronym for the German words "Drachenkurven, überlagert" – Dragon curves overlaid. The plotter drawings show fractal configurations with specifically shaped pictorial elements forming a pattern. Their arrangement is based on the so called "Dragon Curves", discovered in the mid-1960s by NASA physicist John E. Heighway and subsequently studied more closely by a number of researchers. Dragon curves can be created by consecutively folding a strip of paper and then depicting the folds as a sequence of left and right turns. They are self-similar in various sizes and, therefore, belong to fractals, something which became known only subsequently and result from consecutively executed mathematical processes. Dragon curves can be combined and put on top of each other well. They then develop visually interesting areas, which prompt the viewer into processes of shape formation. Thus a new family of ornamental forms emerges, inviting new aesthetic experiments.

Richard Buckminster Fuller

Richard Buckminster Fuller (1895–1983) was an architect, designer, engineer and author.

132–135 The pattern as a loadbearing structure: The groundbreaking use of so-called tensegrity structures – loadbearing structures, which, by balancing compression and tension, are self-stabilising, is the best-known achievement of passionate American researcher Richard Buckminster Fuller. Together with his student Kenneth Snelson, Fuller conducted experiments at the Black Mountain College in North Carolina on dome structures, culminating in the development of the geodesic dome in 1949. Its construction was patented in 1954 and it has since been used en masse for tents in military camps and as the architecture for popular spectacles. A geodesic dome with a diameter of approx. 76 metres was erected for the pavilion of the United States at the 1976 World Expo in Montréal. So distinctive is the dome's appearance that carbon allotropes discovered in the 1990s, bearing some resemblance to the dome structures, were named Fullerenes.

Diane von Furstenberg

The fashion designer Diane von Furstenberg is based in New York.
www.dvf.com
www.therugcompany.info

136/137 Diane von Furstenberg is regarded the inventor of the wrap-around dress, which she had produced in the 1970s from a jersey material. More than five million of this sporty and uncomplicated piece of clothing with its simple cut were sold over a period of just a few years. Different material designs are typical for von Furstenberg's fashion, the patterns of which are created from large, dynamic shapes in brilliant colours. The rug "Spiral Hearts" is one of her designs for The Rug Company.

G

Sarah van Gameren

Sarah van Gameren is a London-based designer.
www.sarahvangameren.com

138/139 "Burn Burn Burn!" Open fire is a subject central to many designs by Sarah van Gameren. This designer from Holland used to experiment in her kitchen with paint that had been enriched with flammable pigments and, once dried, functioned as a painted-on fuse. Decorative traces of fire remain as a result of the pyrotechnic performance.

Poul Gernes

The Danish artist Poul Gernes (1925–1996) initially trained as a lithographer before coming to art as an autodidact. Later, he became the co-initiator of the Copenhagen Experimental Art School, founded in 1961.

140–143 Gernes became known for his series of motifs from the 1960s and 70s, ranging somewhere between the genre of Pop Art and American Minimalism. A decade on, he devoted himself to decorating and designing the interiors of public buildings, such as a 25-storey hospital near Copenhagen. In addition to patterns of stripes in various colours, reminiscent of Scandinavian national flags, the Danish artist often made use of the target pattern and of other circular shapes, also producing them as complex spatial installations, for instance.

Henriette Grahnert

The artist Henriette Grahnert is based in Leipzig.

144–145 Grahnert's large-scale oil paintings appear conventional and monumental only at first glance. Within their confines the artist places stumbling blocks, carefully and sensitively composed, which question the painting's cohesiveness and fragment it. And so her works with the meaningful titles "Ja gesagt, Oh nein gedacht" or "nicht kompatibel" tell of her interest in less important matters. She develops her compositions from traces and residues of the painting process, in which she allows visual elements of an entirely different flavour to meet: a crosswise grid, accurately applied with childlike seriousness, is placed alongside blobs of paint as well as abstract forms and areas.

Hervé Graumann

The artist Hervé Graumann, born in 1963, lives in Geneva.
www.graumann.net

146–151 Hervé Graumann is regarded one of the pioneers of the digital media arts in Switzerland. However, unlike his previous works, Graumann's "Patterns" series was not created on the computer, but composed of real objects from industrial mass production. He pedantically arranges such trivial things as a steel wool scourer, a clothes peg and a horse sculpture made of plastic to form irritating patterns, which he does not present as installations. Even where, in the form of photographs and wallpaper. Even where, in relation to "Patterns", Graumann is working with real objects and such traditional art forms as installations or photography, he remains loyal to the computer. His compositions quote the "wallpapers" that are so popular with computer users as background for their desktops. Like other works by this Swiss artist, his patterns develop their wit and their analytical potential through a transfer from one medium to another. In this case, he transforms the computer users' virtual wallpaper into a real wall covering.

Grazioli Krischanitz ARGE

The two independent architects Alfred Grazioli (born 1940) and Adolf Krischanitz (born 1946) have been collaborating as a working group (in German Arbeitsgemeinschaft, ARGE) on the extension of the Museum Rietberg.
www.graziolimuthesius.de
www.krischanitzundfrank.com

152–155 The Museum Rietberg in Zurich, an art museum for non-European cultures, is housed in several historical buildings. The new extension is hardly visible from the outside: in order to leave the protected park untouched and so as not to compete with the historical villas, the architects chose to build underground.
The only sign of the new building noticeable from within the park is the green glass entrance pavilion. Richly grained onyx was used for the design of the backlit ceiling. Grazioli and Krischanitz then contrasted this natural surface design with a small-scale crystalline pattern that covers all the glass surfaces.

Andreas Gursky

The artist Andreas Gursky was born in 1955 in Leipzig; he is now based in Düsseldorf.

156/157 In the past, Andreas Gursky studied with the photographer couple Hilla and Bernd Becher. Like them, he used a plate camera for his work, not confining himself to architectural subjects, even if these do play a very important role in his works. Gursky became known for large-format tableaux depicting places typical for late capitalist society: factory buildings, mass concerts and apartment blocks as much as the interiors of a luxury boutique or of a 99-Cent-Shop. Making use of wide-angle lenses and of panorama formats, Gursky generates a distanced viewpoint. The documentary nature of his images is undermined, however, by the application of digital image-manipulation techniques, brought into play by the artist in order to, for instance, refine the image composition. At the same time, Gursky emphasises patterns in all of his works. He shows them even where they would not, normally, be perceived, by working in his images without any central objects and treating all details equally through the use of extreme depth of field.

H

Susanne Happle

Susanne Happle, born in 1968, studied design at the Design Academy in Eindhoven and today lives in Marburg.
www.susannehapple.com

158/159 Designing interactive materials is an important area of research; innovations in this field are generally planned by think tanks and developed in laboratory settings. Without any help from research institutions, the designer Susanne Happle was able to devise an application for a very common material. Her concrete tiles "Solid Poetry" react to moisture by displaying an embedded pattern, such as curving lines of flowers. Other patterns and applications for her unusual project are, of course, conceivable.

Heatherwick Studio

The designer Thomas Heatherwick, born 1970, studied design at the Manchester Polytechnic and at the Royal College of Art. As early as in 1994, he established his first studio in London.
www.heatherwick.com

For many years, Heatherwick has been working at the junction of design, art, architecture and engineering. What he does is far removed from smooth product design. His pieces are always technically innovative, like the famous Rolling Bridge at the Paddington Basin, or sculptural, like the enormous sculpture he already affixed to the façade of London department store Harvey Nichols in 1994 as a decoration winding itself through interior and exterior spaces.

160/161 Thomas Heatherwick surrounded the access and parking building Boiler Suit, a part of the Guy's and St. Thomas' Hospital NHS Foundation Trust, with protruding 2.4 metre squares of steel mesh, covering the entire building with a rhythmical surface movement of bulges and depressions. At the same time, these elements fulfil functional requirements insofar as they ensure the building's ventilation and can be easily removed should repairs become necessary.

Britt Helbig

The designer Britt Helbig (born 1983) works and lives in Ghent, Belgium.

162/163 With her wallpaper modules "Wall to Wall" the graphic and textile designer Britt Helbig stages a spatially all-encompassing play on micro and macro perspectives. The wallpaper shows considerably enlarged parts of photographs depicting a piece of weaving.

Matthias Hoch

The artist Matthias Hoch was born in Radebeul in 1958 and studied photography at the Academy of Visual Arts in Leipzig, where he is still based today.

164–167 Matthias Hoch finds the abstract, constructivist forms in his photographs on the streets: in the shape of façades, parking decks or ventilation shafts. From these, Hoch isolates details and changes scale and perspective in order to then combine these everyday elements to series of great formal rigidity. The building structures dissolve and now are but patterns. Were it not for the artist referring to their origins in titles such as "Vatikan #26" or "Brüssel #8", they could not be placed as being from anywhere.

Josef Hoffmann

Josef Hoffmann (1870–1956) was an architect and designer and a co-founder of the Viennese Workshops.

168–171 Alongside buildings, furniture and lighting, Josef Hoffmann's designs include graphics and textiles as well. His covering patterns and material designs show a development moving away from the organic and craft influenced forms of the Viennese Workshops and of Art Nouveau and towards the "geometric abstraction" of Modernity. His designs combine hand finishing with the seriality of mass production.

I/J

Jim Isermann

The artist Jim Isermann was born in Wisconsin in 1955 and today lives in Palm Springs, California.
www.jimisermann.com

In Jim Isermann's work, it is not only the borders between design and art that blur; rather, it is separating the two categories that in fact seems obsolete. With his works he resists not only the traditional notion that design plays, in comparison to art, a subordinate role, but also escapes at the same time today's evaluative criteria in design. His works are not functional and do not produce any commercial advantage, but appear as patterns or simple decoration. So he sews colourful quilts, paints underground railways or decorates façades and balconies. In doing so, the influences of Op Art and of the design from the sixties and seventies – from Verner Panton, for instance – are unmistakable.

172/173 Isermann's interest in spatial staging begins with the wall piece "Vega" (1999). His installations consist of self-adhesive vinyl sheets with glowing colours and large area geometrical forms, which do not repeat themselves, however, according to a strict canon. During an interview about "Vega" in Grenoble, he explained: "I am not interested in random patterns. How strict the repetition of individual elements is, that is very significant for me."

174/175 His design for the hundredth exhibition at the Portikus in Frankfurt conveys a celebratory mood. The silver foil transforms the institution into a festive hall. As in a cabinet of mirrors, the light is reflected from the foil as it falls in. The dots Isermann designed do not present an endless rapport but were conceived for this space with the help of a computer.

K

Kapitza

The German-born sisters Nicole and Petra Kapitza run their design studio in London.
www.kapitza.com

176–179 Nicole and Petra Kapitza have developed a number of image and illustration fonts, which allow designing one's individual patterns with any computer keyboard. In this free typographical way of

working, situated between resource and art project, the font places floral or geometrical forms or silhouettes of animals or humans respectively, depending on which key is pressed on the keyboard.

Klein Dytham Architecture

This studio for architecture and design was established in Tokyo by Astrid Klein and Mark Dytham in 1991.
www.klein-dytham.com

180/181 Within the portfolio of the architects Astrid Klein and Mark Dytham there are a number of projects where the design of level façade surfaces gave the building a distinctive look.
In the case of their Heidi House in Tokyo, fire protection regulations had an influence on the design of the façade. The building is set back from the street and is therefore governed by less strict directives, allowing the architects to construct a plywood cladding for the entire façade, covering it on the outside with glass. Klein and Dytham contrast their rather sober and functional construction style with a pattern of traditional Tyrolean wood cut-outs serving as windows.

182/183 R3 Ukishima/Aicafe54 is a four-unit, elongated building in the town of Naha in the Okinawa province. A 25 metre long and five metre high screen extends along the entire side of the street; behind it is attached a large-scale floral motif. From the outside, the grid of the façade and the pink ornamentation resemble the pixels of rough computer images, while the rays of the sun create a play of light on the inside.

Astrid Krogh

The textile designer Astrid Krogh is based in Copenhagen.
www.astridkrogh.com

184–187 Astrid Krogh has arranged 256 neon tubes to form an automatic pattern generator measuring 2.5 by 7.2 metres and programmed to produce over 100,000 different combinations of form and light. Krogh designed her neon wallpaper "Polytics" for the Danish parliament; for the geometrical shapes of the tubes, Krogh borrowed from a frieze by Rasmus Larsen on display in the central entrance foyer of the parliament building.

Kengo Kuma

The architect Kengo Kuma, born 1954, is a professor at the Faculty of Science and Technology at the Keio University in Japan.
www.kkaa.co.jp

188/189 In addition to large scale projects such as museums and office buildings, Kengo Kuma designs temporary buildings. In the summer of 2007, the architect erected a mixture of igloo and Chesterfield sofa in the garden of the Museum of Applied Arts in Frankfurt/Main. Its large, white body is his interpretation of the Japanese teahouse – as well as a technical challenge. The structure is inflatable, and the precision of its shape surprising. The teahouse, which was only in temporary use, could also be heated, and was furnished with integrated LED lights.

L

Zuzana Licko

The designer Zuzana Licko, born in Bratislava, lives in Berkeley, California.
www.emigre.com

190–193 The typographer Zuzana Licko became known for her typeface label Emigre, a distribution service for digitally designed typefaces, which she established in 1984 together with partner Rudy VanderLans. The firm caused a sensation in the 1980s when it developed new and extravagant typefaces for the then still young market in desktop publishing. Under the same name, Licko and VanderLans published a graphic design magazine, exerting much influence on '80s and early '90s graphic design. At first glance the images of the "Puzzler Prints" series do not seem to have any connection to the work of a typographer. For her compositions, all arranged from circles of varying sizes and density, Licko does actually use the same software that she uses for the development of her font families. Zuzana Licko also finds inspiration in her daily work as a graphic designer, be it in halftone grid photographs, interferences or in the moiré effect of layered grids of dots.

Harmen Liemburg

Harmen Liemburg was born in 1966 and works as a graphic designer in Amsterdam.
www.harmenliemburg.nl

194/195 The patterns on the packaging of Japanese sweets inspired this Dutch graphic designer to create his floral compositions "Crispy Cloud Kombini Crystals" for the Dutch-Japanese cultural institution Siebold House in the Dutch city of Leiden.

196/197 In his poster "Ki Ki Ri Ki", Liemburg superimposes classical motifs of poster history, such as Hokusai's "The Great Wave off Kanagawa" or Bonnard's "France-Champagne", in such a way that a symmetrical pattern emerges. He thus calls attention to the most important representatives of his craft, while, at the same time, making them disappear into the superimposed layers. His unusual compositions with their layerings and repetitions of pictorial motifs were inspired by the technical opportunities afforded in screen-printing.

Michael Lin

The artist Michael Lin was born in Taiwan in 1964. He lives and works in Taipei, Brussels and Paris.

198–201 The patterns from his childhood still inspire Michael Lin today. Now, the artist gives new contexts to the traditional floral decors familiar to him from cushion covers and bedspreads in rural Taiwan. Stylised blossoms and flower buds – blown up beyond proportion – emerge in international museums as expansive installations. The enlarged patterns cover floors, walls and articles of daily use. He makes his motifs appear unfamiliar by frequently reproducing them to such a large scale that, at close sight, they are hardly recognisable, or by placing them bottom side up as he did in his installation for the exhibition "Notre histoire…" at the Paris Palais de Tokyo. In addition to the sheer size of the ornaments, the context which he chooses for his patterns often surprises the viewer. Art or decoration: with Lin, there is no unequivocal answer to this question.

Lydia in St Petersburg

The textile designer Susan Krieger, born 1977, established her company Lydia in St Petersburg while still studying at the University of Art and Design Burg Giebichenstein in the German town of Halle/Saale.
www.lydia-stpetersburg.de

202/203 Susan Krieger specialises in textiles with a metal finish so opulent and lavish that production is only feasible by hand. Bronze or copper is printed in a screen-printing process on silk and other textiles and classic decorative patterns are layered on top of each other in several stages of printing. The reflective qualities of the metal surfaces, alternating with blank areas, create an effect of great depth on the material.

Ane Lykke

Ane Lykke studied at the Danish Academy of Design. Today she is based in Copenhagen.
www.anelykke.com

204/205 Mind the Gap – the in-between spaces are what gives movement to the geometrical patterns by textile designer Ane Lykke. The elements of her installation – tape, honeycomb shapes made from plastic, coloured areas – are arranged in levels and constantly change their appearance, depending on the viewer's perspective.

M

Luna Maurer

The designer Luna Maurer was born in 1972 and lives in Amsterdam.
www.poly-luna.com

206/207 The traditional Argyle knitting-pattern of differently coloured diamond shapes in a checkerboard arrangement results in part from technical limitations imposed on the craft by the first knitting machines. Designers Luna Maurer and Roel Wouters documented what changes occur in the pattern when it is worn as a pullover by a person. The result they then inserted as a flaw in the weave into the Argyle pattern. In doing so, they don't just cause visual irritation, but at the same time highlight innovations in knitting technology. The pullover was produced as a limited edition (10 pieces in five different pattern variations) on a modern industrial machine at the Textile Museum in the Dutch city of Tilburg.

Barry McGee

The artist Barry McGee, born 1966, lives in San Francisco, California.

208/209 In the San Francisco scene of graffiti artists, Barry McGee became known as "Twist", "Ray Fong" and "Robert Pimple" in the early 1990s. After showing his pieces at the 2001 Biennale in Venice, McGee managed to establish himself on the art market and many of his Street-Art pieces were taken down and stolen. In galleries, McGee presented his works framed and arranged to surfaces of greater density, where individual patterns interlock and overlay each other. He applies a similar method to his installation "Advanced Mature Work", directly gluing simple geometrical shapes to the wall and thus creating a form of quilt from the individual sheets of paper.

Michael Meredith

The architect Michael Meredith is an Associate Professor of Architecture at the Harvard University Graduate School of Design.

210/211 The potentially burgeoning "Ivy" coatrack consists of single Y-shaped plastic modules, which can be joined by four unique connector types, forming various three-dimensional structures.

212–215 On the occasion of the 40th anniversary of the Carpenter Center for the Visual Arts at Harvard University, the only building by Le Corbusier in the United States, the French artist Pierre Huyghe devised a piece for puppet theatre in honour of the architect. Michael Meredith created the temporary stage for the play – a tunnel-shaped structure of white diamond shaped plastic modules, overgrown by moss. "There's a critical point in the puppet show where Corb sits under a tree, so I focused on a tree that was on the site. The structure is almost an egg; I describe it as the inside of an eyeball. On one side it frames the tree, and on the other side it frames the puppet show." (I.D. magazine, August 2005)

Igor Mischiyev

The artist Igor Mischiyev was born in 1966 in Moscow and today lives in Berlin.

216–219 In his series "die Zugereisten" Igor Mischiyev works on a ground for his painting that is rich in references and associations: a shiny mattress cover. The interiors depicted on it in watercolour derive from architects and designers of classical Modernity, such as a Paris apartment by Eileen Grey or the Whitney Museum in New York by Marcel Breuer. The search for your homeland in foreign parts is the overarching motif of the series. African masks stand as symbols for leaving your homeland and for the loss of mythological-mystical significance, as well as for being taken over by Modernity, which seems in Mischiyev's subjects to be no more than a representative style of dwelling. The fireplace, which appears repeatedly in the paintings, points to the theme of domestic intimacy and its function as the traditional meeting place of the family or of the clan. The mattress drill he uses reinforces the sense of security and intimacy, but restricts perception of the motifs: the shiny threads, with which the pattern is woven into the material, do not take on any colour, are strongly reflective and make the rooms disappear behind a veil of patterns.

Modulorbeat

Architects Marc Günnewig (born 1973 in Münster) and Jan Kampshoff (born 1975 in Rhede/Westfalia) with their studio Modulorbeat, established in the German town of Münster in 1999, carry out interdisciplinary projects in design and architecture.
www.modulorbeat.de

220–223 Temporary buildings, in contrast to buildings for permanent use, offer good opportunities for experiments. The info pavilion for the 2007 Sculpture Projects Münster makes a fine example for this: it is based on a simple steel grid scaffolding structure erected in several levels, the floors of which are constructed from common construction grade plywood. With the exception of the bookshop, which is protected from the wind and weather on all sides by sheets of lorry canvas, all areas lack solid walls: the casing of the façade, perforated sheets of metal finished with a shimmering gold-coloured copper-aluminium alloy, was directly screwed onto the scaffolding. Once dismantled, these modules were recycled by their manufacturer.

Sarah Morris

The artist Sarah Morris was born in 1967 and lives in London and New York.

224–227 High-gloss paint and square sheets of canvas are constants in Sarah Morris' work as a painter. She devises groups of her works in series, concentrating on a limited number of geometrical shapes and grid structures in constantly changing ranges of colour. Although her paintings are highly abstract, Morris is not so much part of concrete or constructivist art; her works emphasise the narrative element, their titles shedding light on references impossible to gather from the paintings themselves. Her series are named after large cities, for instance, such as Beijing or Los Angeles, from where she captured architectural details. The artist further explains her investigative manner of working in films, in which she presents documentary research as well as narrative and associative material.

Mount Fuji Architects Studio

The Mount Fuji Architects Studio was established in 2004 by Masahiro Harada (born 1973) and Harada Mao (born 1976) in Tokyo.
www14.plala.or.jp/mfas/fuji.htm

228–231 The inspiration for the four-storey residential building Sakura in Tokyo isn't obvious at first glance: Mount Fuji Architects Studio refer to two glass houses famous in architectural history – Farnsworth House by Mies van der Rohe and Johnson House by Philip Johnson. Rather than taking up formal elements in their design, the architects endeavoured to find an adequate translation of the freedom and privacy so characteristic for these transparent glass houses and essentially resulting from, according to Masahiro Harada, their forest surroundings. Harada's solution: two free-standing walls made of sheets of steel, into which a traditional Japanese cherry blossom pattern was punched, shield the building from its environment. Clear volumes create an impressive contrast to the Meguro residential area with its extremely high density of small-scale buildings.

N

Marc Newson

The designer Marc Newson, born in 1963 in Australia, lives in London and Paris.
www.marc-newson.com

232/233 Marc Newson is probably the most sought-after designer of his generation. He has designed almost everything, from watches, furniture and the interiors of cars up to a spaceship. Characteristic of his work are futuristic, bimorphous shapes resembling stream-lined planes or trains. Cooperating with clothes manufacturer G-Star, Newson designed – in addition to jeans – a memorable logo in the form of a large, stylised button. This design recurs in the pattern of the padded jacket. However, only fragments of its shape are visible in its newly arranged rapport.

O/P

Christopher Pearson

Christopher Pearson is a London based designer.
www.christopherpearson.com
www.lookatyourwalls.com

234–237 Christopher Pearson applies new technology to the traditional medium of wallpaper. For his designs, he makes use of the wallpaper patterns by William Morris, founder of the Arts and Crafts Movement in the late 19th century. Pearson interferes with the motifs by animating miniscule elements of the design, which, at irregular intervals, begin to move. Pearson's manipulations leave room for associations, representing a subtle form of media production.

Pipa

The designer Pipa lives in London.

238/239 Large-scale graphical patters form the common element in the "Wearables" series, a fashion concept consisting of clothing fabric and printed posters, thereby including the wearer in the design experiment.

Q/R

Tobias Rehberger

The artist Tobias Rehberger was born in 1966 in the German town of Esslingen. He studied art at the Städelschule in Frankfurt, where he lives today.

240–243 The concept artist Tobias Rehberger translates into his work the pursuit of functionality and appropriate form familiar from design and architecture. He makes use of the formal language of design and creates objects which appear functional – such as a three-dimensional structure that could be the cladding for a façade as much as a room divider and which, irritatingly, is made of dental plaster. Rehberger adds to this game of contextual approaches suggestively narrative titles like "Utterances of a quiet, sensitive, religious, serious, progressive, young man, who presumes from his deep inner conviction that he is serving a good cause".

Bernd Ribbeck

Bernd Ribbeck was born in 1974 in Cologne and today lives in Berlin.

244–247 Ribbeck is one of the younger representatives of concrete painting, though carrying out his work with the tools of a graphic artist. In his small formats, which resemble the avant-garde of modernist abstraction in particular, Ribbeck combines watercolours and other paints applied on wood or canvas with unusual tools like ballpoint pens or markers. While he refrains from choosing titles, all traces of his work remain, even the structural outlines for his colour-field painting.

Clare Rojas

The artist Clare Rojas was born in 1976 and lives in San Francisco, California.

248–251 Clare Rojas' paintings, with their clean colours and accurately delineated detail smacking of folk art and seemingly naïve, are characterised by their own narrative form reminiscent of fairy tales, comic strips and votive pictures, and combining formal elements belonging to these genres. In this, the artist assigns a key role to geometric shapes: they appear to fulfil supernatural functions. Crystals and geodesic domes appear where one would need the powers of a superhero or where mysterious events occur.

S

Savant

The Savant fashion label was founded in 2007 by David Gensler and Aerosy-Lex Mestrovic in New York.
www.svsv.net

252–255 Savant is part of the luxury clothing brand Serum VS Venom (SVSV). The label's knitwear collection made of Mongolian cashmere is modelled on historic patterns from the Arabian cultures.

Annette Schröter

Annette Schröter, born in 1956 in the German town of Meissen, is a professor of painting at the Academy of Visual Arts in Leipzig.

256–259 In her work, the painter Annette Schröter time and again turns towards paper silhouettes. In many cultures and in countries such as Poland, China or Switzerland, paper cutting is a traditional craft. Schröter uses this technique in her rounded cuts, but instead of the usual ornaments, she employs patterns of company logos such as those of Deutsche Bank or Lufthansa. Furthermore, Schröter creates richly ornamented portraits of stereotypical figures like the heroic socialist worker or of a veiled "woman under arms" from paper cuts the size of tapestries or church windows.

Yinka Shonibare, MBE

The artist Yinka Shonibare was born in 1962 as the child of Nigerian parents in London and spent his childhood in Lagos, Nigeria. Later he studied in London, where he still lives today.

260–263 Yinka Shonibare describes himself as "truly bi-national". And with his works, he shows what that means. He adapts so-called African fabrics and their patterns into Victorian-inspired robes or interiors.
Particularly the richly and gaudily patterned clothes, which are presented on headless mannequins in many of his installations, have a complicated and multifarious history. The materials, as he found out, are also known as "Dutch Wax" and originate from Indonesia, where the Dutch colonial rulers discovered the local batik techniques for industrial production. But it was finally the British, who produced these textiles in Manchester and took them to West Africa. Only in the 1960s did the fabrics and their patterns become popular on the Dark Continent as a sign of African independence and identity. "And it's the fallacy of that signification that I like," says Shonibare. "It's the way I view culture – it's an artificial construct." Besides cultural identity, Shonibare's work also deals with subjects like social affiliation and eroticism. In the film "Un Ballo in Maschera" and in the installation of the same title he shows, in allusion to Verdi's opera, the murder of King Gustav III of Sweden at a masked ball in 1792 as an ambivalent game of sexual identity and aristocratic lifestyle. Ultimately, masks and costumes traditionally imply the possibility to try out new roles and to allow for erotic adventure respectively.

Katrin Sonnleitner

The designer Katrin Sonnleitner was born in 1976 in the German town of Erlangen. She lives in Karlsruhe.
www.katrin-sonnleitner.com

264/265 For centuries Persian rugs have been knotted by hand in a laborious process. The arrangement of the differently coloured knots creates the ornamental pattern of the rug. The "Persian Puzzle Rug" combines the craft of knotting with the fashion: with fairly little skill and effort, it is possible to arrange one's own rug. Everybody can decide which ornament they prefer and where it should be placed. A rubber backing on the bottom side of the individual pieces gives the faux-Persian rug stability.

Esther Stocker

The artist Esther Stocker was born in 1974 in South Tyrol and now lives in Vienna.
www.estherstocker.net

266–269 Esther Stocker's works are black and white without exception. Her motifs are geometrical grid structures which leave the viewer without orientation and seem to stretch space into infinity. Her spatial installations in particular, created according to the same principle, cause great irritation. Small, intentionally included "flaws", which repeat and form their own patterns, further emphasise this effect.

Christine Streuli

Christine Streuli, born 1975, is an artist based in Switzerland. In 2007 she was one of the artists invited to exhibit in the Swiss Pavilion at the Venice Biennale.

270–273 Christine Streuli calls herself an impatient and fast worker. Clear and swift decision making, therefore, characterises her art. She works with a palette knife, she cuts and sprays on ornaments such as stars or patterns. Her preferred way of applying paint is indirect, without coming into contact with the canvas at all. She also makes use of techniques like monotyping, or she works with printing blocks that equally serve fast working and do not leave any traces of a paintbrush. In 2007 at the Swiss pavilion of the Biennale in Venice she exhibited her works in the form of a spatial installation.

Studio Job

Job Smeets (born 1970 in Belgium) established the design practice Studio Job in Antwerp in 1998. In 2000, his partner Nynke Tynagel (born 1977 in the Netherlands) joined the successful design studio.
www.studiojob.nl

The two designers, having trained at the renowned Eindhoven Academy, are known for their painstakingly handcrafted cast bronze objects and other individual pieces. They often decorate their large fairy-tale like sculptures with ornaments that are as lavish as they are profound, their imagery being reminiscent of comic strips and logos.

274/275 The pair created the "Insect Patterns", crawling with bugs and other creepy-crawlies, for the Dutch designers Viktor & Rolf.

276/277 For the hotel restaurant Matbaren, Studio Job designed a golden wall screen with an irritating mixture of death's heads, axes, nuclear power stations, as well as birds and cloud ornaments. The provocative picture makes a cynical contrast to the otherwise cosy and stylish atmosphere of the Grand Hôtel Stockholm.

Richard Sweeney

Richard Sweeney is a designer and lives in Huddersfield in the UK.
www.richardsweeney.co.uk

278/279 When constructing his complex paper sculptures, Richard Sweeney restricts himself to simple materials and tools. Although he grooves, cuts and glues by hand, his modules appear as perfect as if a computer had generated them. Photographs are an essential element of this designer's work and photographed objects are almost as important to him as the sculptures themselves. Sweeney finds inspiration for his work in science and in traditional Japanese origami.

T

Jon Thompson

The artist, author and curator Jon Thompson was born in 1936 and lives in Brussels.

280/281 Jon Thompson's sequence of works, "Valletta", is a typology of hand-painted dot grids in varying colour combinations. A comparison reveals subtle differences between the images: The rhythm of the dots is interrupted on the horizontal and on the vertical axis, creating a cross shape and thereby dividing the image into four areas. The dots that were applied evenly fade into the background.

Karsten Trappe

Karsten Trappe studied graphic design and now works as an artist in the German town of Braunschweig.

282–287 Processes of movement are at the centre of Trappe's work. He measures the oscillations of a pendulum, feeds the data to a computer and obtains a filigree pattern of accurately linking circles. This pattern documents the earth's movement, the gravitation and kinetic energy involved as well as the timing of the movement.

U

Aya Uekawa

The artist Aya Uekawa, born in Tokyo in 1979, now lives in New York.
www.ayauekawa.net

288–291 Aya Uekawa positions figures with mask-like faces all looking equally expectant in environments of symmetrical ornaments or in two-dimensional cityscapes. She simultaneously calls upon very different epochs of art history: the faces of her figures remind you of medieval altar paintings as much as of manga, and in the background of her picture, she quotes the imagery of Op and Pop Art.

Patricia Urquiola

Patricia Urquiola, born in 1961 in the Spanish city of Oviedo, studied architecture and now manages her own design studio in Milan.
www.patriciaurquiola.com

292/293 The architect Patricia Urquiola earned an international reputation as furniture and interior designer. Her designs are characterised by comfort and cosiness and are always sensual and experimental. Urquiola's installation for the "ideal house cologne" at the imm cologne, an international trade fair for furnishing, demonstrated her vision for tomorrow's residences and at the same time served the designer as an archive of objects she is interested in. Traditional patterns from various cultures play a central role here. Urquiola's designs reflect her eclectic way of working, showing a broad spectrum of forms and influences from different craft traditions rather than a signature style.

294/295 Urquiola completed some of her most famous designs in collaboration with the Italian furniture manufacturer Moroso, such as the lounge chair "Antibodi" with its petal ornamentation.

V

Henrik Vibskov

Henrik Vibskov initially worked as an artist and musician. After studying at the Central Saint Martins College of Art and Design in London, he founded a fashion label under his own name in Copenhagen in 2001.
www.henrikvibskov.com

296–301 Henrik Vibskov is a busy pop star who knows how to use the catwalk as much as museums and clubs as a stage. His men's fashion collections showcase Vibskov's talent for eclectic combinations and are a commentary on as well as a caricature of the fashion industry. "The Fantabulous Bicycle Music Factory" for instance, his 2008 spring/summer collection, blends large scale patterns from different cultures with cut-off suit trousers. It is only consistent then that Henrik Vibskov, as a parody on the Western view of the indigenous peoples whose patterns and way of dressing he quotes, has his models appear in blackface.

Miguel Vieira Baptista

Miguel Vieira Baptista, born 1968, is a designer and lives in Lisbon.
www.mvbfactory.com

302–303 Miguel Vieira Baptista's modular carpets Figo and Mancha allow their owner to choose: by means of a colour fan one can compose the colours of hexagonal modules according to one's liking. In addition, both carpets can be laid out in the room like islands, complete with cavities for coffee table and floor lamp. The carpet tiles were produced in a limited edition.

W

Kelley Walker

The artist Kelley Walker was born in 1969 in Columbus, Georgia. Today he lives and works in New York.

Kelley Walker's works address questions of authenticity and authorship, consumption and taste. Walker makes references by means of images from media and advertising that he appropriates for his work and through his choice of materials: instead of paint, Walker might for instance apply chocolate or toothpaste. The artist occasionally sells his works as digital image files, ready to be appropriated further and recontextualised.

304/305 The Marantz record player represents the musical taste and listening habits of a generation that grew up in the 1970s. Kelley Walker piles up the abstract symmetrical pattern where, usually, there would be a vinyl record. By so altering the record player advertisement, the artist evokes mandalas as well as psychedelic patterns.

306/307 Walker's piece "Maui" is based on the picture of a plane crash in Hawaii already shown on the cover of "Colors", a magazine published by fashion company Benetton. Walker overlays it with a grid of coloured dots, in reference to the company slogan "United Colors of Benetton".

Marius Watz

The artist Marius Watz (born 1973) lives in Oslo, where he also teaches. He initiated the platform generator.x, which gives protagonists of generative art (computer art) an opportunity for exchange.
www.unlekker.net

308–311 Marius Watz was only eleven years old when he started working with the computer. In 1993 he dropped out of his computer studies course at University in order to design graphics for techno-raves. Ever since he has been concerned with generative systems for creating visual form, still, animated or realtime. His organic and colourful forms have earned him a reputation in the field. Today, he belongs to the best-known exponents of generative art.

Bernhard Willhelm

Born in Ulm in 1972, Bernhard Willhelm studied fashion design in Antwerp and today runs a studio in Paris.

312–315 Bernhard Willhelm's fashion does not conform to the mainstream. His creations are more mask and disguise than wearable fashion. He combines traditional pieces, such as local costume and uniforms with elements from the world of theatre, fairy tale or comics into a peculiar, witty-ironic sign system. Spirits and ghosts inhabit his collections as do seamen in striped pullovers or types in Bavarian lederhosen. Willhelm does not recognise such a thing as bad taste: "Just a twist or another perspective and it can just as well count as good taste."

Mette Winckelmann

The artist Mette Winckelmann lives in Copenhagen.

316–319 Mette Winckelmann's colour field works are based on national flags. Their strict principles of spatial division – into thirds, into halves, the golden mean – are taken over by Winckelmann and extended ad absurdum, until small areas of surface remain. The artist thus works with colour just as she does with monochrome, finely textured textiles, which she sticks onto canvas. She complements her constructivist way of working with expressionist elements: the colour scheme moves away from the clear signal colours of the flags; their surfaces are not geometric but dynamic free-hand forms, which bring movement into her work and are only seldom accompanied by template forms and contrasted with them.

X/Y

Michael Young

Michael Young was born in 1966 in Sunderland, England. Today the designer runs his own studio in Hong Kong.
www.michael-young.com

320/321 Michael Young's concept for the interior design of the cosmetic surgery clinic of Dr James in Taipei shows a concentration on luxurious furnishings, innovative materials and the most modern technologies, all in keeping with the object itself. Young took his experiments with CNC-cut Corian further and collaborated with Katrin Olina who designed the graphic patterns for the back-lit Corian panelling. He also developed the furniture together with prestigious firms like Cappellini or Poltrona Frau.

Z

Toby Ziegler

The artist Toby Ziegler lives in London.

322–325 Toby Ziegler designs the motifs for his pictures on a computer. He manipulates photographs, overlays them with vector sketches from geometrical forms and arranges them with elements, which have the typical gesture of 3D simulations and virtual worlds. These unusual compositions, which you can read as classical subjects from art history, like still lives and landscapes, serve Ziegler as blueprints for large-scale painting. He carefully transfers his sketches, a process in which every detail rapidly generated by synthesis – through the brushstroke or also by overlaid gold leaf – can change its character.

About the Editors

The interior architect **Barbara Glasner** works as a consultant and freelance curator for design and architecture in Frankfurt am Main. In the context of her collaboration with the German Design Council from 2001 to 2007, she supervised the various editions of the design project "ideal house cologne" where internationally renowned designers present their vision for living in the future, for the International Furniture Fair Cologne.

Petra Schmidt is a freelance author and design consultant in Frankfurt am Main. She teaches design theory at the Karlsruhe University of Arts and Design and writes for magazines such as "art" and "Frame". After studying media science in Frankfurt, she worked for various design companies and was the editor-in-chief of the design magazine "form" from 1999 to 2007.

Ursula Schöndeling works as an academic associate at the Kunstverein Braunschweig. She studied art history in Frankfurt am Main and, as a freelance author and curator, has planned publications and exhibition projects for, among others, the Oper Frankfurt, the atelierfrankfurt and the Revolver publishing house, also in Frankfurt.

A Note of Thanks

We owe special thanks to the artists, designers and architects involved. We are also grateful to all the photographers, who generously made their images available to us. Furthermore, we wish to thank all the museums, art associations and galleries, who assisted us in our search for image material.

Hunting for images, ideas and good manuscripts is a complex business. We thank all those who supported us on our journey: **Helge Aszmoneit** Frankfurt/Main, **Cornelia Durka** Berlin, **Karianne Fogelberg** Frankfurt/Main, **Friedhelm Hütte** Frankfurt /Main, **Véronique Hilfiker Durand** Basel, **Katrin Tüffers** Frankfurt/Main, **Violetta** und **Natalie Walter** Neu-Isenburg, **Markus Weisbeck** Frankfurt/Main, **Mirko van den Winkel** Udine, **Markus Zehentbauer** Basel.

The editors
Barbara Glasner, Petra Schmidt, Ursula Schöndeling

Photo Credits

Richard Allan/Andy Tan 232/233
Moderna Museet Stockholm/Per Anders Allsten 94/95
Daici Ano 14/15, 26–29, 182/183
Thorsten Arendt/Artcoc.de 222/223
Ryota Atarashi 180/181, 228–231
Frans Barten 116/117
Jürgen Baumann 115
Anders Sune Berg 312–315
Primoz Bizjak 268
Bernd Borchardt 288
Zooey Braun 43
Luis Silva Campos 302/303
Vivien Chen 320/321
Sylvia Diamantopoulou 20–23
Torben Eskerod 184–187
Thom Faulders Architecture 118–121
David Franck 42
Sarah van Gameren 138/139
Wolfgang Günzel 174/175, 240–243
David Heald 72–77
Claus Helmut 55
Andreas Ilg, Zurich 270–273

Thomas Jautschus 113
Ilmari Kalkinen 150/151
Matthias Knoch 144/145
Alex Kohout 80–83
Panos Kokkinias 24/25
Willi Kracher 152–155
Kravets/Wehby Gallery 290/291
Dorte Krogh 204/205
Achim Kukulies 246
Ingmar Kurth/Constantin Meyer 292/293
Mathias Langer, Braunschweig/Varel 49
Bart Van Leuven 163
Nicolas Lieber 146–149
Lydia in St Petersburg 202/203
MAK/Georg Mayer 170/171
Satoru Mishima 122–125
Frederik Molenschot 158/159
Thomas Müller/Kunstverein Braunschweig 140–143
Tim Nighswander 16–19
Linka Odom 46/47
Cristobal Palma 68–71
Martin Pardatscher 266
Sameli Rantanen 92/93

Christian Richters 45, 220/221
Marcus Schneider 112, 114
Erasmus Schröter 256–259
Studio Eye, Udine 294/295
Edmund Sumner 160/161
Richard Sweeney 278/279
Nic Tenwiggenhorn, Berlin 99, 100
Joep Vogels 206/207
Josh White 89–91
W. Woessner 267, 269

We have taken pains to locate all copyright holders. Should we have not been successful in individual cases, copyright claims should be addressed to the publishers.

Imprint
Patterns 2. Design, Art and Architecture
Barbara Glasner, Petra Schmidt, Ursula Schöndeling (eds)

Editor: Karianne Fogelberg
Editorial Contributors: Cornelia Durka, Markus Zehentbauer
Translation: Anja Welle, Stan Jones, Berlin, Hamilton (NZ)
Graphics: Surface Gesellschaft für Gestaltung mbH
Katrin Tüffers, Markus Weisbeck
Production: Lithotronic Media GmbH, Dreieich

This book is also available in German:
"Patterns 2. Muster in Design, Kunst und Architektur", ISBN 978-3-7643-8643-6.

Library of Congress Control Number: 2008923156

Bibliographic information published by the German National Library
The German National Library lists this publication in the Deutsche Nationalbibliografie;
detailed bibliographic data are available on the Internet at http://dnb.d-nb.de.

© 2008 Birkhäuser Verlag AG
Basel · Boston · Berlin
P.O. Box 133, CH-4010 Basel, Switzerland
Part of Springer Science+Business Media

© 2008 for the reproduced works vested in their originators and their legal successors.

Printed on acid-free paper produced from chlorine-free pulp. TCF ∞

Printed in Germany

ISBN: 978-3-7643-8644-3

9 8 7 6 5 4 3 2 1
www.birkhauser.ch